CLIL

Dive Deep into Japanese Culture

Yukiko Ito

Hazuki Nakata

Nicole Marie Takeuchi

Kazuko Kashiwagi

Chief editor :
Shigeru Sasajima

SANSHUSHA

はじめに

　本書は、CLIL (Content and Language Integrated Learning)（内容と言語を統合した学習）の考え方をもとに構成してあります。単なる英語学習ではなく、日本の伝統文化・伝統工芸を実践的に考え、英語と日本語を使って伝えられる力を培うことを目標にしています。CLIL を通じて英語を使うことを学んでください。

　CLIL は、文化社会や科学などの内容を英語や日本語などの言語と統合して学ぶことです。ヨーロッパでは標準的なカリキュラムとなり、日本でも次第に浸透してきています。

　CLIL では、学ぶ内容 (Content) があり、内容と関連して思考 (Cognition) し、内容や思考をもとにコミュニケーション (Communication) しながら、文化の違う相手に理解したことをどうやって伝えるかを工夫 (Culture) します。これは「4つの C」(4Cs) として知られる CLIL の基本理念です。学習者の母語も適切に使うことが大切です。

　現在でも、私たちの日常生活と深く関係している文化や工芸を題材として取り上げています。日本の伝統的な文化や工芸を単なる知識として学ぶだけはなく、日本文化を深く理解し探究してほしいと願っています。「絵ろうそく」「風呂敷」「俳句」「水引」「カレー」「発酵食品」などは私たちの身近にあるものです。また、「なまはげ」「三線」「空手」などはよく知られていますが、その背景や成り立ちなどはあまり知らないのではないでしょうか。昨今、レトロとして注目を集める「マジョリカタイル」についても取り上げます。

　これらの題材を通して、日本の伝統文化や伝統工芸について考え、英語で伝え、英語で話し合い、世界の多様な文化や工芸について共有できることを願っています。

　英語は多少むずかしい部分もありますが、気軽に英語と日本語の両言語をうまく使う工夫 (translanguaging) をして、互いに「意味を伝える (negotiation of meaning)」ことに集中してください。英語力は、CEFR 6レベルの A2 程度（英検準2級程度）を想定していますが、それ以上でもそれ以下でも、間違うことを恐れず、お互いに助け合いながら (scaffolding)、CLIL の活動を楽しんでもらうことを期待します。

春を待つ　木々のつぼみは　たおやかに

Waiting for spring now Flower buds on the trees are Graceful and flexible

著者一同

本教科書の構成

　題材は、Picture Candles, The Furoshiki, The Namahage, The Sanshin, Haiku to the World, Mizuhiki, Japanese Curry, Karate, Fermented Food, Mallorca Tiles を選びました。また、Column Travelogue in Japan として、著者が実際に訪ねた場所の様子や伝統工芸を具体的に紹介しています。

　各 lesson は以下に示す構成と活動となっています。それぞれの学習活動は、興味に応じて柔軟に考えてください。CLIL で大切なことは多様性と柔軟性、自律的に学ぶことです。どの lesson から始めてもかまいません。興味ある内容をさらに深めてください。

活動（タスク）	活動の展開例など
1 Warmup talk	冒頭の導入部分の英文をもとに、学習者同士で英語と日本語で話す活動です。内容に興味を持つことが目的です。
2 Keywords	題材内容と関連する語句をまとめてあります。例文を暗唱するなどして活用してください。
3 Dialogue	題材内容と関連する短い会話を提示しています。ペアで会話し、それをもとに自由に話題を広げてください。
4 Activity	題材内容と関連する活動を提示しています。各活動を英語を使いながらすると効果的です。
5 Background knowledge	題材内容の理解を深める文章を読む活動です。日本語に訳すことではなく、内容を理解し次の活動などに発展できるように読んでください。
6 Research	2つの task に沿って話し合いながら調べる活動です。調べ方のプロセスを楽しんでください。
7 Creating	創造的思考 (creative thinking) を培う活動です。実際にものを作ったり、作曲するなど、学習するだけではなく、実践することを目的とします。巻末の Worksheet を活用してください。
8 Presentation	Creating の活動を発表する活動です。
	最後に reflection で、自分自身の学習をふりかえります。クラスメートと共有して次の学習につなげましょう。

Column については、日本のさまざまな伝統文化と伝統工芸について考える題材として、グループワークをするなど、自由に活動してください。

Contents

Lesson 1 Picture Candles
絵ろうそく

🔊 01 **美しい絵が描かれた絵ろうそくを知っていますか？**

Do you know much about Japanese picture candles, which have been used in Japan since ancient times? There are many types of candles in the world. In recent years, reasonable western candles are used most often in our daily lives. That is because they burn **longer than** Japanese ones. Their flames last **longer**, though the size of the flame is **smaller**. The Japanese picture candle, however, is a traditional handmade candle that produces a beautiful, flickering flame.

1 Warmup talk 英語で話してみよう

例　A: What are the characteristics of Japanese picture candles?
　　B: Well, they are made from plants, right?

🔊 02 ## 2 Keywords 英語でどう言えばいいの？

伝統工芸	There are many **traditional crafts** in Japan.
和ろうそく	**Japanese candles** may burn shorter than western candles.
ハゼの実	Japanese candles need wax obtained from **the goby fruit**.
みつ蝋	**Beeswax** is made from the hives of honeybees.
ぬか蝋	My sister loves to use **rice bran wax** candles at home.
木蝋	**Wood wax** candles are popular for relaxation.
イ草	**Soft rush** is a plant used to make tatami mats.
ろうそくの芯	**Candle wicks** are made of rushes soaked in oil.
揺らめく炎	A **flickering flame** is a feature of Japanese picture candles.
パラフィン	**Paraffin** wax is often applied to our hands and feet.
仏壇	Many Japanese homes have a **Buddhist altar**.

🔊 03 ③ Dialogue 役割を決めてやってみよう

A: Come on in, Matty.

B: Thanks, Yuma. Wow! That's a big Buddhist altar.

A: Yes, it is. It's my family's traditional altar.

B: What's this? Is it a candle with a picture on it?

A: It's a Japanese picture candle. The candlemaker paints these flowers on it.

B: A Japanese picture candle? It looks **thicker** and has a **bigger** flame **than** the candles I know.

A: Yes, they are thick. They are a traditional Japanese craft.

B: Wow, I've never seen them before. It's a waste to use these picture candles, isn't it?

A: Well, why don't you take one home and put it on your desk?

④ Activity 絵ろうそくに使う花の名前を知ろう

例のように、次の花の名前がどの絵か話し合ってみよう。

> 例
>
> A: The flower in this picture is *sakura* in Japanese. What do you call this flower in English?
>
> B: I call it a cherry blossom.

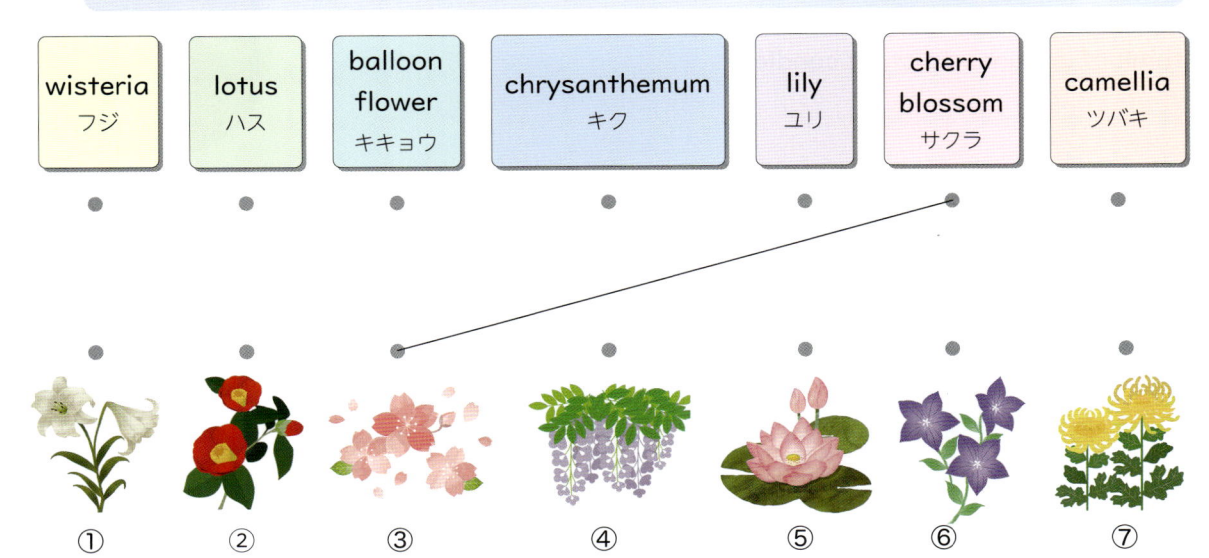

| wisteria フジ | lotus ハス | balloon flower キキョウ | chrysanthemum キク | lily ユリ | cherry blossom サクラ | camellia ツバキ |

① ② ③ ④ ⑤ ⑥ ⑦

flickering flame

stays litt

a Japanese candle   a Western candle

We have long used candles in our daily lives. When candles are offered at a Buddhist altar, they are usually accompanied by flowers. However, in cold regions such as Tohoku and Hokuriku, winters are long and there are few flowers that bloom. So, it is said that people began to draw images on candles. Picture candles were already sold at candle shops in town during the Edo period. They were often decorated with flowers such as peonies and chrysanthemums. They were very expensive and were used only by samurai families. Today, picture candles are a popular traditional Japanese craft among visitors to Japan.

Japanese candles have various characteristics. First, they are made from plant materials such as wood wax made from the goby fruit, beeswax, and rice bran wax. Next, they produce less oily smoke, and their wax doesn't drip. Also, their candle wicks are made of soft and thick rush, soaked in oil, and used for the core of the candle. The flames flicker widely and don't go out. That is partly because they are made by hand. The Japanese candle is now a precious commodity, so naturally it is expensive.

On the other hand, western candles are made from paraffin wax, so people can buy them at a reasonable price. They have **thinner** wicks **than** Japanese candles and they burn **longer**. Western candles are used widely these days, while Japanese candles are rarely used in daily life. Which do you like to use, western candles or Japanese candles? What do you think of Japanese picture candles?

True or false?　ペアで内容を確認しよう

1. Japanese candles are made from paraffin wax.
2. Since Japanese picture candles are made by hand, they can't be mass-produced.

例 A: Is it true or false?
   B: It's true, because … / It's false, because …

6 Research　絵ろうそくについてもっと知ろう

絵ろうそく (picture candles) は、古くから作られている和ろうそくに絵を描いたものです。和ろうそくの歴史や作り方などを、本やウェブサイトで調べてみましょう。

参照例

本

　『伝統と美と技　和ろうそくの世界』（大石孔他著、文葉社）

　『和ろうそくは、つなぐ』（大西暢夫著、アリス館）

安堵町歴史民俗資料館

ウェブサイト

　Candles – *Warosoku*

　What are *Warosoku*? 6 Things to Know about Japanese Candles

　山形県ふるさと工芸品

　松井本和蝋燭工房

　手仕事にっぽん　和ろうそく

　灯芯ひき技術　奈良県安堵町

Task 1　ろうそくの特徴を表にまとめてみよう

	Japanese candles	Western candles
materials	plants	paraffin
wicks	**thicker**	**thinner**

Task 2　例のように和ろうそくについて自分の考えを話してみよう

1. I found that Japanese candles have many different designs, and some have modern pictures, such as those for Halloween.

2. I would like to draw my favorite design on a Japanese candle.

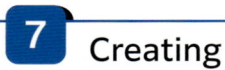
和ろうそくにカラーペンで絵を描いてみましょう。季節の花や、クリスマスやお正月など季節の行事をデザインしたものも人気があります。

How to make picture candles:

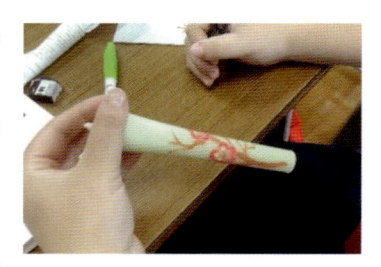

1. Decide on the theme of your picture candle and the flowers you want to draw.
2. Draw on the candle using marker pens, acrylic paint, etc.
3. Paint the candle, starting with the lightest color.

4. After it dries, paint a second coat to make the color darker.
5. When finished, show your candle to your friends and explain why you chose that design.

用意するもの：和ろうそく、カラーペン、アクリル絵の具など

Hello everyone. I am Tomo. Today I would like to talk about my design idea for a picture candle. I like sunflowers, so I painted them on my candle. The flower language of sunflowers is "passion." I would like to challenge various things with passion. Sunflowers are **larger** and **more powerful than** any other flower I know. That's why I love them. Thank you for listening.

Presentation Phrase Building 1

- Hello everyone. I am Tomo.
- Today I would like to talk about ～.
- Thank you for listening.

みなさん、こんにちは。私はトモです。

今日は、～についてお話しします。

聞いてくれてありがとうございます。

プレゼンテーションの原稿を書いてみよう

Reflection: Self-assessment (A = 100 – 70% B = 69 – 40% C = 39 – 0%)

Content	Language
A B C	A B C

Reflect on your learning in English.　英語でふりかえりをまとめよう

Lesson 2 The Furoshiki
風呂敷

🔊 05 風呂敷は何かを包む布ですが、なぜ「風呂敷」と書くのでしょうか？

The *furoshiki* is a highly convenient cloth in Japanese culture. Just one piece of fabric can wrap various items. However, why is it **called** *furoshiki*? Or why is it **written** as 風呂敷 in Chinese characters? Let's study the history and use of the *furoshiki*.

---

1 Warmup talk　英語で話してみよう

例　A: Do you know what the origin of the word *furoshiki* is?
　　B: I'm not sure. Please tell me.

🔊 06 ## 2 Keywords　英語でどう言えばいいの？

奈良時代	Buddhism developed in the **Nara period**.
舞楽	*Bugaku* is a traditional art combining dance and music.
将軍	Tokugawa Ieyasu was the most powerful **shogun**.
幕府	The Ashikaga **shogunate** ruled from 1336 to 1573.
行商人	**Traveling merchants** sold food at town markets.
持続可能な代替手段	*Furoshiki* have been used as **sustainable alternatives**.
小売業者	Amazon is the world's largest online **retailer**.
ポジャギ	*Pojagi* is a Korean cloth used to wrap, carry and store things.
チマチョゴリ	*Chima jeogori* is a Korean national costume for women.
結び	There are many types of **knots** for tying a *furoshiki*.

3 ## Dialogue　役割を決めてやってみよう

A: Oh no!

B: What's wrong?

A: I thought I had **brought** my eco bag, but I forgot it. It's a hassle to queue at the checkout again to buy plastic bags. It's a long queue. I don't have anything to put my shopping in.

B: Oh no! I don't have one either. Oh wait, let me see... Ah, here it is. Here you go.

A: What's this? A cloth? A scarf?

B: It's a *furoshiki*. It's a cloth **used** in Japan to wrap things.

A: Really? But if you wrap two wine bottles, they might hit each other and break.

B: It's okay. A *furoshiki* is versatile, so leave it to me.

4 ## Activity　風呂敷の柄について知ろう

次の風呂敷の柄はどの説明に合っているか話し合ってみよう。

唐草（からくさ）	矢絣（やがすり）	宝尽くし	青海波（せいがいは）
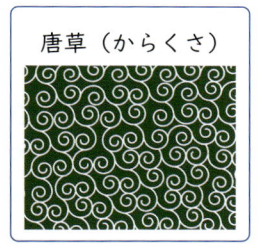	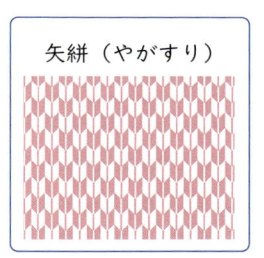		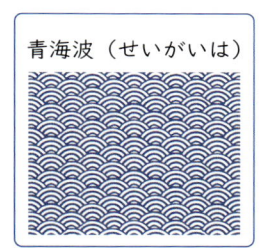

① The endless wave pattern carries wishes for eternal happiness and the desire for people's peaceful lives to continue into the future.

③ The pattern **inspired** by vines spreading in all directions was **introduced** to Japan through the Silk Road. This design **depicting** vines expanding, symbolizes longevity and prosperity, **making** it an auspicious pattern.

② The design expresses the feathers of birds like hawks or eagles **attached** to the upper part of an arrow. The arrow, **symbolizing** hitting the mark, has been traditionally **used** as an auspicious pattern.

④ The design is **filled** with seven treasures: a key, a treasure scroll, a **hidden** raincoat, a **hidden** hat, a weight, a money pouch, and a cross.

The *furoshiki* is a Japanese wrapping cloth. It is one piece of fabric, but it is much more than that. It can be a design, an artwork, or a craft, and it is a piece of Japanese history.

The oldest **existing** *furoshiki* dates back to the Nara period, when it was used to wrap costumes for *bugaku* or a Japanese classical dance. The *furoshiki* gained its name during the Muromachi period. Later, they were **used** as floor coverings in public bathhouses, and then for wrapping clothes during bathing. According to history records, when Ashikaga Yoshimitsu, the 3rd shogun of the Ashikaga shogunate, built a large public bath, guests used their *furoshikis* decorated with family crests to wrap their clothes.

In the Edo period, the *furoshiki* became essential to traveling merchants. For example, merchants from Toyama carried *furoshiki* **adorned** with retailer names when **traveling** and **selling** medicine all over Japan. The *furoshiki* was a good advertisement.

The *furoshiki* has recently gained renewed attention due to environmental

concerns. Plastic pollution in the oceans has become a global issue, leading to **increased** calls for **reducing** plastic waste. In response, Japan implemented a plastic bag fee in July 2020. The *furoshiki*, with its portability, versatility, and reusability, has been used as a sustainable alternative.

Do you have any *furoshiki* at home? Do you sometimes use them? Do you know there are many different styles and designs of *furoshiki*? They are sold at gift shops, grocery stores, department stores, or online retailers. Why not use *furoshiki*? They are very convenient.

True or false?　ペアで内容を確認しよう

1. The people began to use *furoshiki* when bathing in the Muromachi period.
2. *Furoshiki* are eco-friendly items to reduce plastic waste.

例 A: Is it true or false?
　 B: It's true, because … / It's false because …

6 Research 風呂敷についてもっと知ろう

世界の包む文化について調べてみよう。

The *furoshiki* has many different patterns and colors, each of which has a special meaning. Let's look into what these patterns and colors mean. In old comics and cartoons, thieves often carried *furoshikis* with a certain pattern **called** arabesque. However, arabesque patterns are **considered** to be very lucky because they symbolize something that cannot be **cut** or **interrupted**. So, why are arabesque patterns a symbol for thieves?

Wrapping culture is not unique to Japan. In our neighboring countries, such as South Korea, there is something **called** *pojagi*. Let's explore wrapping cultures around the world.

Task 1　風呂敷のように布の多様な使い方について調べてみよう

Name	Procedure	Characteristic	Place
pojagi	It was made by piecing together leftover fabric from making clothes.	patchwork	Korea

I (We) found the *pojagi*. It is a traditional Korean cloth made by women. It is leftover fabric from making clothes such as *chima jeogori* (*Hanbok*). Pieces of fabric are created by patching and stitching. Using leftover fabric this way is an important part of Korean traditional culture.

Task 2　風呂敷のような布を 1 つ選んで紹介してみよう

風呂敷の結び方や包み方を工夫してみよう。

❶ *Ma-musubi*（真結び square knot）

It is a type of knot that doesn't come undone easily once it is **tied**, but when you want to untie it, it can be undone quickly.

❷ *Futatsu-musubi*（2つ結び two-knot）

You use this method when an item is long and the length of one *furoshiki* is not enough.

❸ *Sao-tsutsumi*（竿包み Pole wrapping）

This is a wrapping method for bundled long and thin items. This wrapping method ensures that the item remains tightly **wrapped** without the risk of it **sticking** out or **shifting** inside.

❹ *Suika-tsutsumi*（スイカ包み Watermelon wrapping）

This is a convenient way to wrap round items, such as watermelon or a ball.

❺ *Bin-tsutsumi*（瓶包み：2本 2 bottle wrapping）

This is a wrapping method for two bottles, such as wine bottles or one-shō bottles (approx. 1.8 liters). It's *advisable* to adjust the size of the *furoshiki* **based** on the size of the bottles.

写真提供：むす美

Hello, everyone! I'm Akio. Today, let's discover a unique way to wrap round items. First, center the item on the *furoshiki*. Next, tie a square knot at the front, forming a loop for your hand. Repeat at the back. Then, hold both knots, pass the front knot through the back loop, creating a handle. Finally, pull the upper knot up, and you can carry a round item with you. Thank you for your attention!

Presentation Phrase Building 2

- Let's discover a unique way to 〜.
- Thank you for your attention!

〜というユニークな方法を見つけよう。
ご清聴ありがとうございました。

プレゼンテーションの原稿を書いてみよう

Reflection: Self-assessment (A = 100 – 70% B = 69 – 40% C = 39 – 0%)

Content			Language		
A	B	C	A	B	C

Reflect on your learning in English. 英語でふりかえりをまとめよう

Travelogue in Japan　にほん伝統工芸紀行①

Kabazaiku is made from dried mountain cherry bark.
樺細工はヤマザクラの樹皮を乾かして作ります。

Urushi takes about a week to dry.
うるしは乾くまでに一週間くらいかかります。

　日本には北から南まで各地に素晴らしい伝統工芸があり、これらの地を訪れ、それぞれの工芸を体験することができます。そのような日本各地の伝統工芸を紹介します。

　雪深い冬の間、家で過ごすことが多い東北地方ではさまざまな伝統工芸が生まれました。武家屋敷で知られる秋田県角館市は「樺細工」が有名です。樺細工は江戸時代に武士の内職として育まれました。幹から丁寧に剥がし、乾かした山桜の樹皮を使って、アクセサリーや茶筒などを作ります。角館で

樺細工体験

樺細工コースター

伝統工芸士に樺細工コースターの作り方を教わりました。温めたコテを使って板に、細かい模様を切り抜いた桜の樹皮を押し付けるように貼っていきます。樺細工は、すべて天然の素材でできた素朴で温かい工芸品です。

　岩手も工芸品の多いところです。平安時代末期、奥州藤原氏三代、藤原秀衡が建築した世界遺産、中尊寺金色堂が有名な平泉市には「秀衡塗」という工芸品があります。金箔を組み合わせて装飾し、縁起のよい草花が、うるし絵で描かれているのが特徴です。秀衡塗は素朴ながら華麗な味わいを見せています。平泉ではうるし塗りに挑戦しました。うるしは塗った後、乾くまで一週間くらいかかりますが、それを利用して加飾が可能となります。うるしには、樹液にウルシオールという成分が含まれていて、その美しさとは裏腹に、触るとかぶれます。慎重さが求められる大変細かい作業が必要です。他にも秋田の曲げわっぱ、岩手の南部鉄器や宮城の伝統こけしなどがあり、東北地方は伝統工芸品の宝庫ですね。

秀衡塗（うるし塗）体験

秀衡塗のお椀 © 伝統工芸　青山スクエア

Japanese Traditional Crafts

Task What craft are you interested in? Share ideas with your classmates.

曲げわっぱ

Akita is famous for *magewappa*. These bentwood containers are made using the bark of Akita cedar and mountain cherry trees. They have a long history, as they have been discovered in ancient ruins. Craftsmen thinly peel the natural Akita cedar and carefully select pieces with beautiful grain to create these containers.

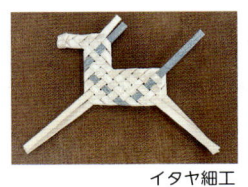
イタヤ細工

Itaya-zaiku in Kakunodate City, Akita, has more than 200 years of history. *Itaya-zaiku* has been made mainly for farming tools or toys. This *itaya* horse can be hung not only as a wall decoration, but can also be made to stand with its legs spread out to the side.

南部鉄器瓶

Iwate is famous for its *Nambu tekki*. It is made from *sentetsu* (iron). This photo shows a simple and sturdy *Nambu tekki*. It is fired at a high temperature of about 900 degrees Celsius to prevent rusting.

箱根寄木細工

In Hakone, Kanagawa, there is a craft called *yosegi-zaiku*. It involves gathering different colored pieces of wood together to create patterns. By changing the color scheme and the type of wood, many different patterns can be created. The beautiful patterns created by craftsmen are characteristic features of this craft.

日光下駄

In Nikko, Tochigi, there is a lot of snow, so the *Nikko geta* was invented in the Edo period. They are manufactured by sewing *zori* to *geta* soles. They are cool in summer and warm in winter.

アイヌ刺繍

The Ainu, who have lived for centuries in Hokkaido, embroider various patterns on their clothing and other items. Ainu patterns include a spiral pattern called *Moreu* and a pointed pattern called *Aiushi*.

Lesson 3 The Namahage
なまはげ

🔊 10 秋田県の伝統行事なまはげについて知ろう。

There are ogres called Namahage in Japan. They appear on New Year's Eve and visit local families in Akita to find children who aren't behaving well. Typically, Namahage are either red or blue. This photo shows their faces. Do you want to see the real Namahage?

JR 秋田駅のなまはげ

---

1 Warmup talk　英語で話してみよう

例　A: What do Namahage usually wear when visiting local families?
　　B: I think they wear *wara*-coats.

🔊 11 2 Keywords　英語でどう言えばいいの？

なもみ	*Namomi* refers to red blisters on a person's hands and feet.
先立 （さきだち）	*Sakidachi* lead the way for Namahage.
ケデ	*Kede* is a type of raincoat made of straw and linen.
出刃包丁	*Deba-boucho* is a large knife.
巾木 （はばき）	Namahage wear straw shin guards called *habaki*.
わらぐつ	Namahage wear a pair of straw boots called *waragutsu*.
手桶 （ておけ）	Namahage have a pail called *teoke*.
無形文化遺産 （むけいぶんかいさん）	There are 22 **Intangible Cultural Heritage** items in Japan.
悪い子はいねが〜	**Are there** any naughty children here?

3 Dialogue　役割を決めてやってみよう

🔊 12

A: Where did you travel for the holiday, Kaito?

B: My family traveled to Oga in Akita and saw the Namahage tradition on New Year's Eve.

A: How did you like it? I have never seen the real Namahage event.

男鹿真山伝承館（秋田）

B: It was very cold, but I felt like I was experiencing Japanese traditional culture.

A: Really? Please tell me about it.

B: OK. **There is** a Namahage mask I bought in Akita. I will show it to you and the Namahage videos.

4 Activity　なまはげを体験しよう

🔊 13

役割を決めて演じてみよう。

On New Year's Eve. The Namahage are walking around the town.

Sakidachi: Good evening. I'm here to tell you that the Namahage are coming soon.

Father: Good evening. Thank you. We were waiting for you.

Namahage: **Are there** any crying children here? **Are there** any naughty children here? Take them into the mountains!

The Namahage enter the house and walk around, shouting and making loud noises.

Father: Thank you for coming. Please enjoy some delicious food and sake.

Namahage: Thank you. How is your family doing?

All the family members gather around the Namahage.

Father: We all worked very hard this year. We were not lazy.

Namahage: Really?

Father: Sure. They all worked very hard and studied a lot.

Namahage: I heard that **there are** some kids that are always playing computer games.

Mother: No! They always helped their grandfather and grandmother.

Namahage: OK. Your family has been in good health, right?

Mother: I broke my leg, but I'm fine now.

Namahage: Good. **Are there** any naughty children here?

Children: No. Not at all.

Namahage: **Are there** any crying children?

Children: Oh no! We're scared but we aren't crying.

Namahage: OK. I'll be back next year! See you then.

The Namahage event is an annual event which takes place on New Year's Eve in the Oga region of Akita. The 'Oga no Namahage' belong to a type of *Raiho-shin* that wear masks and costumes. *Raiho-shin* are visiting Gods. They were given Intangible Cultural Heritage status by UNESCO in 2018.

The word "namahage" comes from *namomi hagi*, which means to peel red blisters. In the past during the winter months, most people in Akita spent a long time sitting around the fire and developed blisters on their hands and feet. *Namomi hagi* implied avoiding bad behavior. Over time, the word *'Namomi hagi'* became the Namahage.

The Namahage look scary, but that's not all that they are. They can be heartwarming, too. On New Year's Eve, the Namahage visit each family in villages, while shouting and making loud noises. The Namahage ask how they have been over the past year. When they find some children they shout at them, "**Are there** any naughty children here?" They are scared of him and swear they'll be good for the coming year. The village's younger adults take turns being the Namahage and carrying on the tradition.

宮古島のパーントゥ © 宮古毎日新聞

There are other traditional *Raiho-shin* similar to the Namahage in other places in Japan. For example, Miyako Island has the *Paantu*. They go around the houses smearing mud, making loud noises, and chasing children.

ドイツのクランプス

Not only Japan, but parts of Europe also have similar customs with masks and costumes called a *Krampus*. *Krampus* wears hand-carved masks with long horns and fur capes, and parades through the streets making loud noises. It warns naughty children, brings good luck, and blesses couples that have children.

True or false?　ペアで内容を確認しよう

1. The Namahage were registered as UNESCO Intangible Cultural Heritage in 2018.
2. Does *Krampus* go around the houses smearing mud?

例 A: Is it true or false?　B: It's true, because … / It's false, because …

来訪神 (Raiho-shin) は UNESCO で次のように無形文化遺産として紹介されています。来訪神については、「文化庁遺産オンライン」などで調べてみよう。

「来訪神：仮面・仮装の神々」

Raiho-shin rituals take place annually in various regions of Japan — especially in Tohoku, Hokuriku, Kyushu, and Okinawa — on days that mark the beginning of the year or when the seasons change.

例 甑島のトシドン (*Koshikijima no Toshidon*)

写真提供：薩摩川内市

Task 1 来訪神について調べて表のようにまとめてみよう

Name	Place	Mask	Costume
Oga no Namahage	Akita	*Oni* (ogre) mask	*Kede*

Task 2 来訪神を 1 つ選んで簡単に紹介してみよう

例

1. I (We) found that each Namahage mask has a different face and character. All are handmade. They are very attractive.

2. I (We) would like to see how real Namahage visit local houses in Akita on New Year's Eve.

怖くて優しいなまはげのお面を自分で作ってみよう。出来上がったお面をつけて、なまはげの世界を体験しよう。

How to make a Namahage mask:

❶ Choose the materials.

❷ Draw the shape.

❸ Draw holes for the eyes and mouth.

❹ Cut out the eyes or mouth.

❺ Don't cut out the full mask, leave some extra paper around the shape.

❻ Add color to the mask with markers, crayons, and paint.

❼ Add some decorations: e.g. glitter, jewels, and feathers.

❽ Cut the mask out fully.

❾ Attach strings or rubber bands on both sides for ties.

❿ Let the mask dry, then put it on.

用意するもの：厚紙、色画用紙、ハサミ、のり、ガムテープ、毛糸、輪ゴム、カラーペンなど

Hello everyone. We are Group 1. I'm Kakeru. Today, we'd like to talk about *Krampus*, a famous Christmas visitor in some parts of Europe. Look at this picture. *Krampus* warns naughty children and wishes people good luck. *Krampus* and Namahage have one thing in common: they wish people a happy life. I found these traditions very interesting. Thank you for listening. Do you have any questions?

Presentation Phrase Building 3

- We are Group 1.　　　　　　　　　　　　私たちは１班です。
- Have you heard of *Krampus*?　　　　　クランプスについて聞いたことはありますか？
- I found these traditions very interesting.　とても興味深い伝統だと思いました。

プレゼンテーションの原稿を書いてみよう

Reflection: Self-assessment (A = 100 – 70% B = 69 – 40% C = 39 – 0%)

Content			Language		
A	B	C	A	B	C

Reflect on your learning in English.　英語でふりかえりをまとめよう

Lesson 4 The Sanshin
三線

🔊 15 **三線や琉球音階を知っていますか？**

The sanshin is a musical instrument from Okinawa. It **is used** in various genres of *Ryukuan* music. The sanshin consists of three main parts: the neck, the body, and the tuning pegs. It **is categorized** into different types based on the shape of the neck. There are seven types of sanshin named after master craftsmen. The *Ryukyuan* musical scale **is** often **used** by Okinawan musicians. The sanshin is an important musical instrument for them.

---

1 Warmup talk　英語で話してみよう

例　A: The sanshin is the same as the shamisen, isn't it?
　　B: They may be similar, but I think they are different.

🔊 16 2 Keywords　英語でどう言えばいいの？

音、音符	The traditional Western music scale consists of seven **notes**.
楽器	The sanshin is a traditional **musical instrument** from Okinawa.
音楽の伝統（遺産）	Okinawa has a rich **musical heritage**.
探求する	That musician **explores** musical scales, rhythms, and melodies.
琉球音階	**The *Ryukyuan* scale** is often used in Okinawan music.
うま	The ***uma*** is a small bridge that holds up the sanshin strings.
ばち	The ***bachi*** of the sanshin comes in a variety of shapes and sizes.
エイサー	***Eisa*** is a traditional folk dance performed in Okinawa.

3   Dialogue   役割を決めてやってみよう

A: Wow! That's cool. Are you playing the shamisen?

B: No, this isn't a shamisen. It's a sanshin.

A: Really? Sanshin? It's different from the shamisen? What's different?

B: Well, look at this. The *bachi* is different.

A: *Bachi*? That's a pick used for plucking the strings, right?

B: That's it. The *bachi* for the shamisen **is shaped** like a ginkgo leaf. But people often use a buffalo horn–shaped *bachi*.

A: Can I try playing it? It looks interesting.

B: Sure. Here you are.

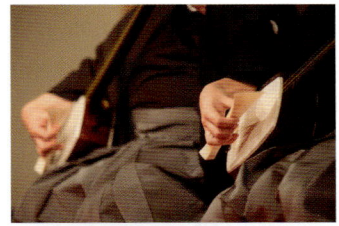

4   Activity   日本の伝統的な楽器を知ろう

次の楽器について質問にそって考え話し合ってみよう。

①    ②    ③

1) What are the names of these Japanese (*Ryukyuan*) musical instruments?

2) How old are they?

3) When and where were they first played?

4) Which of them do you want to play?

5) Japan has many traditional musical instruments. Present one instrument as in the example below.

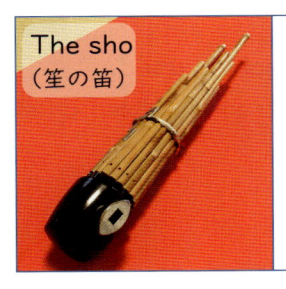 The sho （笙の笛）	The sho is a instrument used in the *gagaku* (Japanese traditional court music).	It was used during the Heian period. The beautiful sounds of the sho make the audience feel they are experiencing something sacred.

The sanshin is a three-stringed musical instrument, like the shamisen. The sanshin **is used** in Okinawan music. Different from the shamisen, it has a *habu*-snakeskin patterned body and wooden neck. When you play the sanshin, plucking strings while pressing down on the notes on the neck of the instrument, you will hear different sounds than the shamisen.

When playing the sanshin, first place it on the right side of your lap and stand an *uma* between the strings and the top of the sanshin body. Next, hold up the edge of the neck called *sao* with your left hand, straightening your back. Then, wrap a *bachi* around your index finger, holding it with your thumb and middle finger to pluck the strings of the sanshin. The music is closely related to *Eisa* or the traditional Okinawa dance.

The Western music we often listen to is rooted in seven musical scales: Do Re Mi Fa Sol La Ti. They are also represented as C D E F G A B or 1 2 3 4 5 6 7. The equivalent musical scales in Japan are expressed as Ha Ni Ho He To I Ro. This method of symbolizing sound is known as solfège. The most well-known use of solfège is "Do-Re-Mi" from the movie *The Sound of Music*. *Ryukyuan* music scales, which are specific to Okinawa, follow the pattern: Do Mi Fa Sol Ti, without the Re and La sounds.

You know some popular Okinawan folk songs, such as "Asatoya Yunta," "Haisai Ojisan," and "Shimancyu nu Takara." Do you like them? They have become elements in J-POP.

True or false?　ペアで内容を確認しよう

1. The sanshin is similar to the shamisen but a different bachi **is used**.
2. *Ryukyuan* music scales from Okinawa are different from Western music scales.

例 A: Is it true or false?
　 B: It's true, because … / It's false, because …

6 Research 三線についてもっと知ろう

三線には、各部位の名前があり、7つの型があります。詳しく調べてみよう。

Look at the picture. The sanshin **is composed** of three main parts: a body (*dou*), a neck (*sao*), and three tuning pegs (*karakui*). Each part has more detailed parts as the picture shows. And there are seven types of sanshin, which are determined by the shape of the neck. Each type of sanshin is named after a master craftsman from the Ryukyu Kingdom era.

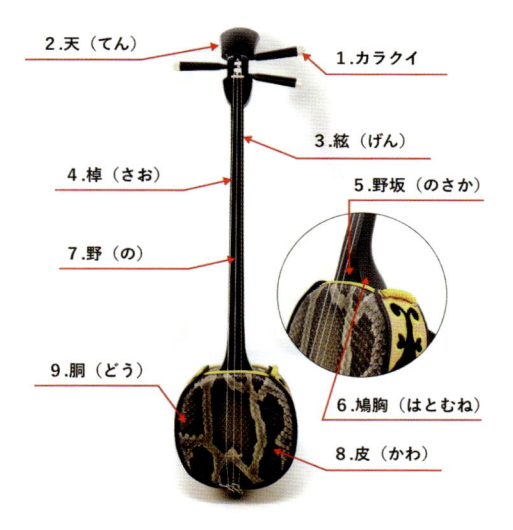

2.天（てん）
1.カラクイ
3.絃（げん）
4.棹（さお）
5.野坂（のさか）
7.野（の）
9.胴（どう）
6.鳩胸（はとむね）
8.皮（かわ）

写真提供：三線職人の専門店 米須三線店

(1) 南風原（フェーバル）型
(2) 知念大工（チニンデーク）型
(3) 久場春殿（クバシュンドゥン）型
(4) 久葉の骨（クバヌフニー）型
(5) 真壁（マカビ）型
(6) 平仲知念（ヒラナカチニン）型
(7) 与那城（ユナグシク）型
　　出典：沖縄県三線製作事業協同組合ホームページ
　　＊その他にも Web では7つの型の情報があります。

Task 1　7つの型の三線の特徴を英語で表にまとめよう

Name	Characteristics	Image
The Haebaru (Febaru) type	This is the oldest type among the seven sanshin types. It is characterized by a slender and compact neck.	

写真提供：沖縄県三線製作事業協同組合

Task 2　7つの型の三線から好きなものを1つを選んで、特徴や選んだ理由をまとめよう

例
> I like the Makabi type of sanshin. It has a beautiful design. When reading the websites about the sanshin, I think that many people would select this type. The *makabi* is very popular. I would like to play this sanshin.

沖縄の音楽は聞いただけで沖縄を思い起こさせます。その沖縄の音階（琉球音階）を使って作曲してみよう。

The *Ryukyuan* scale is a musical scale found throughout Okinawa Prefecture and the Amami Islands of Kagoshima Prefecture. It excludes the notes Re and La which are found in the Western musical scale. It consists only of the notes Do, Mi, Fa, Sol, Ti. This scale, similar to Japanese folk songs and traditional music, is characterized by its five tones.

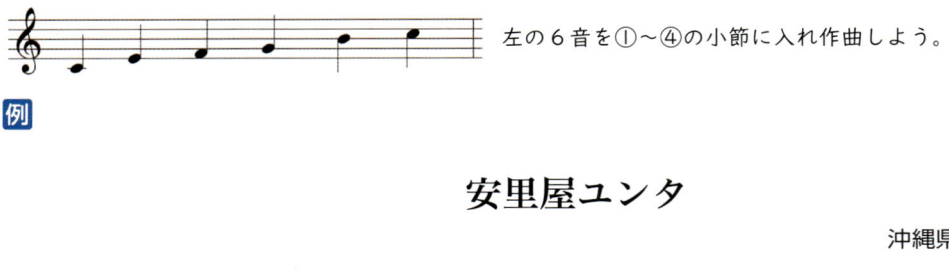

左の６音を①〜④の小節に入れ作曲しよう。

例

安里屋ユンタ

沖縄県民謡

Hello, everyone! I'm Akio. I'm very happy to be able to introduce a song I've composed today. I love playing the sanshin because it has a unique and soothing sound. I created this song with the beautiful beaches of Okinawa in mind. I used simple chords and rhythms on the sanshin to create a tranquil atmosphere. Now, please listen.

Presentation Phrase Building 4

- I'm very happy to be able to introduce ～ .　　～を紹介できることを光栄に思います。
- Now, please listen.　　では聞いてください。

プレゼンテーションの原稿を書いてみよう

Reflection: Self-assessment (A = 100 – 70% B = 69 – 40% C = 39 – 0%)

Content		Language	
A B C		A B C	

Reflect on your learning in English.　英語でふりかえりをまとめよう

Travelogue in Japan　にほん伝統工芸紀行②

Chusenzome is characterized by not fading.
注染染めの特徴は、色あせないことです。

Tin is a soft, bendable and convenient metal.
錫は柔らかくて曲げられる便利な金属です。

注染手ぬぐい

注ぎ染め作業

手ぬぐいの長さを揃える器具

　大阪市の南に隣接する堺市に、「注染染め」という伝統工芸があります。注染では折りたたまれた50枚の生地の、染色したい部分に糊で「土手」を作り、その中に染料を注ぎ込んで染めていきます。表裏両面から同じ柄で染色するのが特徴です。注染の手ぬぐいは、色がにじんだり揺らいだりして優しい色合いになります。そして何度洗ってもほとんど色あせないので、長く使うことができます。染め上がった手ぬぐいは、写真のような専用の器具を使って長さを揃え、ハサミで一気にカットします。すると、素敵な手拭いの出来上がりです。

　富山県高岡市は錫や銅の器で知られています。高岡銅器と呼ばれる器は、原型を作って溶かした金属を流し込んで製作します。錫の特性を生かした「曲がる食器」も有名です。高岡市の錫の器を作る工房で食器の製作を体験しました。木枠に砂を押し固めて鋳型を造型する「生型鋳造法」で、焼いたり乾燥させたりせず、生のまま鋳造するのでそう呼ばれます。この枠に232度に溶かした錫を流し込みます。錫はすぐに固まる性質があります。固まったものをやすりで研磨すれば、錫の器の完成です。

鋳物製作体験

Japanese Traditional Crafts

Task What craft are you interested in? Share ideas with your classmates.

奈良墨

Sumi ink for calligraphy was introduced to Japan from China and Korea around the year 710, and has been made in Nara ever since. Even today, 90% of all *sumi* ink in Japan is made in Nara. The oldest *sumi* ink in Japan is kept in the Shosoin. Nara *sumi* is beautiful, high quality purplish-black and it has a clear aroma.

奈良うちわ

Nara *uchiwa* are gorgeous and very practical. Influenced by Buddhism, Nara *uchiwa* have several different designs such as Nara's scenery, deer, and Shosoin cut into them. Their frames have about 60 to 80 bamboo bones, more than twice as many as other *uchiwa*. However, the fans are very light and create a gentle yet firm breeze.

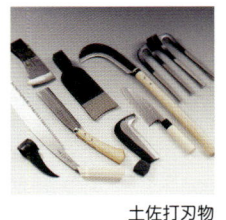
土佐打刃物
© 伝統工芸 青山スクエア

Tosauchi hamono are knife blades made in Kochi. The blades are made through "free forging," a manufacturing method in which knives are shaped by hammering instead of using molds. Japanese swords are also made through this method. The history of *Tosauchi hamono* is said to be more than 400 years. A school has been established to train *Tosauchi hamono* craftsmen.

岡崎石

Okazaki stonework, in which stone is processed to form lanterns and other objects, began in the Muromachi period and has continued since. There are six parts: a ball, a hat, a firebox, a receiver, a pillar, and a ground ring, each of which is carved and assembled into a single piece.

注染手ぬぐい

Chusenzome is a craft from Osaka. In the dyeing process folded cloth is covered with glue, and dye is poured over the surface. The characteristic of *chusenzome* is that it is dyed on both sides of the cloth. Since the dye doesn't fade easily, *chusenzome* stays beautiful for a long time.

錫の器

Toyama is known for its tin and copper. Takaoka copperware is made by pouring molten metal into a mold. Tin is so soft that it is famous as bendable tableware. Plates can be made into any shape.

Lesson 5 Haiku to the World
俳句

俳句は世界でもとても短い詩で、英語でも俳句は作られています。

Haiku became a popular form of poetry at the end of the Muromachi period. Eventually, in the 17th century, haiku came to have the theme of fun and humor by the contribution of Matsuo Basho (1644-1694). He spent his entire life traveling around places such as Tohoku, talking to local people and composing poems. He also incorporated the sense of *wabi-sabi* into haiku. The rhythm of '5-7-5' mora **has pleased** many people in Japan.

CC0 1.0 Universal Public Domain Dedication

In modern times, '5-7-5' syllables in English used for haiku **has become** known around the world.

---

1 Warmup talk　英語で話してみよう

例　A: Do you know *kigo* or seasonal words for haiku?

　　B: Yes. Let me see, *mangetsu* or full moon. It's an autumn *kigo*.

🔊 21 2 Keywords　英語でどう言えばいいの？

季語	Haiku usually uses **seasonal words**.
句会	We will have **a haiku gathering** next Saturday.
機微	Matsuo Basho expressed the **subtleties** of everyday life.
解釈	**Interpretation** of haiku can vary from person to person.
隠喩	**A metaphor** can help understand a concept with a few words.
体言止め	It is sometimes effective **to end a haiku with a noun**.
切れ字	A *kireji* or **cutting word** such as '-kana' brings a lingering effect.
音節	Straw-ber-ry consists of three **syllables**.
母音	A syllable has at least one **vowel** sound in the English language.
拍	In the Japanese language, each *kana* corresponds to a **mora**.

3   Dialogue   役割を決めてやってみよう

A: Hello, Anna.

B: Hi, how long **has it been**?

A: It's been a long time. It **has been** very cold lately for spring.

B: I feel the same. It's time for the cherry blossoms to bloom. In Japan, we call it the season surrounded by cold cherry blossoms.

A: Does that mean "*HANABIE*" in Japanese?

B: Where did you learn such an expression?

A: I learned haiku in Japanese class, so the word came to my mind and it fits.

B: You use the language more sensitively than many Japanese people. That's wonderful. Would you like to join us for a haiku gathering under the cherry blossoms sometime? I'll get you some Japanese paper called *washi*, a calligraphy pen, and some sandwiches.

A: That sounds great! I'll bring hot green tea.

4   Activity   俳句に使われる音を知ろう

それぞれの音を想像して、どの季語がどの絵に合うか話し合ってみよう。

A:（花火の音）This is the sound of fireworks. It reminds me of a *yukata*.

B: That's right. Many fireworks festivals are held in summer.

| fireworks | wind chime | waterfall | bush warbler | temple bell | the sound of insects |

①   ②   ③   ④   ⑤   ⑥

summer

_____ _____ _____ _____ _____

Donald Keene, who was born in New York in 1912, moved to Japan and introduced Japanese literature to the world. He wrote a book about Japanese haiku and translated Japanese haiku into English. His English translation features descriptions of emotion-evoking scenes. Thanks to him, haiku **has become** known as a form of short poetry around the world.

Donald Keene

Here are some tips for creating haiku. First, it is common to use seasonal words in your haiku in order to create vivid images. Second, it is good to use metaphors and noun phrases to create a great rhythm in your haiku. A metaphor can help readers understand concepts with a few words such as 'the taste of rain.' And a kireji such as '-kana' leaves a lingering effect. However, you don't need to be too sensitive about the details. Recently, there **have been** many refined haiku written in a variety of languages on the websites. Why not try to compose haiku in English?

Haiku can help to make you more aware of English phonology and rhythm as well. There are different types of haiku in English. For instance, some do not include seasonal words, and others aren't strict about the number of syllables. By exploring the features of haiku, we can develop a deeper awareness of language.

Compare the following English haiku, which are translated from original famous haiku in Japanese. Do you know which is which? How different are English and Japanese haiku? Which do you like, English or Japanese haiku?

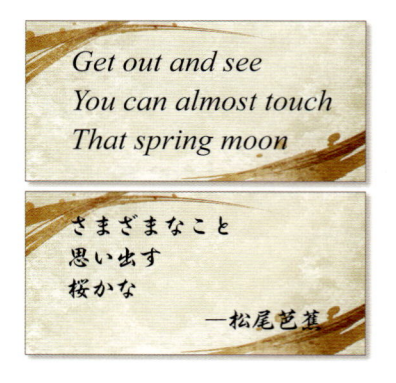

Get out and see
You can almost touch
That spring moon

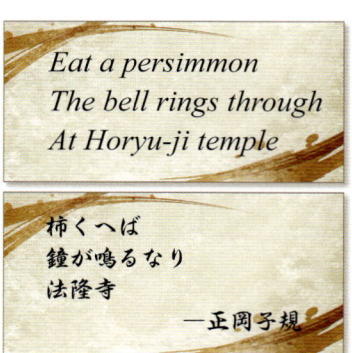

Eat a persimmon
The bell rings through
At Horyu-ji temple

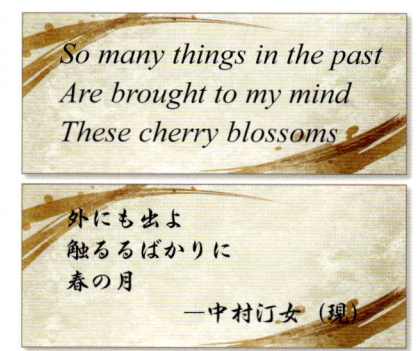

So many things in the past
Are brought to my mind
These cherry blossoms

さまざまなこと
思い出す
桜かな
　　　　　　　　—松尾芭蕉

柿くへば
鐘が鳴るなり
法隆寺
　　　　　　　—正岡子規

外にも出よ
触るるばかりに
春の月
　　　　　　—中村汀女（現）

True or false? ペアで内容を確認しよう

1. The rules of haiku in English are less strict than those in Japanese.
2. Every language has the same system of phonology and syllables.

例 A: Is it true or false? B: It's true, because … / It's false, because …

6 Research 俳句についてもっと知ろう

日本語では、「さ（sa）し（shi）す（su）せ（se）そ（so）」というように拍（mora）を単位として数えます。俳句の5・7・5は拍で数えます。それに対して、英語の音節（syllable）は、基本的に母音（vowel）を単位として数え、「book（1音節）」「Eng/lish（2音節）」という数え方を使います。このような違いは、私たちに言語の面白さに気づかせてくれる機会を与えてくれます。

When writing haiku in Japanese, you just count the morae. However, writing for English haiku, you will have to think about the syllables. This is very useful for understanding languages and developing language awareness.

Task 1 次の俳句 (haiku) について音節と拍を確認し話し合いましょう

| English syllables　5-7-5 |

Sakura all bloom
Shining pink in spring with joy
Petals in my hair

| 日本語の拍　5-7-5 |

古池や
蛙飛び込む
水の音

Task 2 次の有名な俳句を英語にして、グループで較べてみよう

閑さや　岩にしみ入る　蝉の声　　　―松尾芭蕉
やせ蛙　負けるな一茶　これにあり　―小林一茶
目には青葉　山ほととぎす　初鰹　　―山口素堂
兄以上　恋人未満　かきごおり　　　―黛まどか（現）

例　赤い椿　白い椿と　落ちにけり

かわひがしへきごとう
―河東碧梧桐

A red camellia
With a white camellia
Fell to the ground

cf. 英語の俳句ウェブサイト
The Haiku Foundation: https://thehaikufoundation.org/

英語の俳句を作りましょう。作った俳句は例のように紙に書き、句会（haiku gathering）をしましょう。それぞれの句の感想も英語で書いて句会で発表しましょう。

How to write a haiku in English:

Basic rules: e.g.,

- Walk in nature and brainstorm ideas.
- Take notes of your observations.
- Confirm the haiku format: 5 syllables, 7 syllables, and 5 syllables.
- Use seasonal words.
- Use metaphors and noun phrases to create a good rhythm.
- Write the haiku on *washi* paper using a calligraphy pen.
- Share all haiku in groups or with online tools (e.g., Padlet).

例 カナダの生徒（13歳）の俳句

Leaves fall from the trees
A fall breeze blows through my hair
Pumpkin Spice Latte

例 コメント

- I like this haiku. I can imagine autumn in Canada. The part about Pumpkin Spice Latte is wonderful. I would like to have one in Canada. Thank you.
- It's a good haiku. I have never visited Canada. What is autumn like there? However, 'leaves,' 'a fall breeze,' and 'pumpkin' are appropriate words for autumn.

Hello everyone. I am Anna. Today I would like to introduce my own Haiku. "Leaves fall from the trees A fall breeze blows through my hair Pumpkin Spice Latte." A good point of my haiku is that I use pumpkin flavor as a seasonal word. The season of autumn leaves has yet to arrive. Having a latte is comfortable outside in the breezy air. It is the season for small worries to fly away.

Presentation Phrase Building 5

- Today I would like to introduce my ～ .　　今日は、私の～について紹介します。
- A good point of my ～ .　　～の良い点は～。

プレゼンテーションの原稿を書いてみよう

Reflection: Self-assessment (A = 100 – 70% B = 69 – 40% C = 39 – 0%)

Content			Language		
A	B	C	A	B	C

Reflect on your learning in English.　英語でふりかえりをまとめよう

Lesson 6 Mizuhiki
水引

🔊 24 **水引を知っていますか？水引は和紙をこより状にして糊をつけ、乾かして固めて作ります。**

Have you ever used a gift envelope when giving a gift to someone? **It is a good idea to use** a beautiful gift envelope. Look at this, and you see a gorgeous paper craft. It is called mizuhiki in Japanese. Mizuhiki is a craft made by delicately knotting Japanese *washi* paper. History says mizuhiki has been used since Ono no Imoko brought it back from China.

1 Warmup talk　英語で話してみよう

例　A: Do you know which mizuhiki is used for a gift envelope?
　　B: What's that? I don't know what that is.

🔊 25 2 Keywords　英語でどう言えばいいの？

祝儀袋	People in Japan use **a gift envelope** with mizuhiki.
受け継ぐ	The crafts have been **handed down** from generation to generation.
職人	There are fewer **craftsmen** or **artisans** left in Japan.
結納	The *yuino* is a Japanese traditional engagement ceremony.
水引細工	I love **mizuhiki art** works, so I wear them every day.
アクセサリー	There are many types of fashion **accessories** in the world.
立体的な	I like creating **three-dimensional** paper crafts.

3　Dialogue　役割を決めてやってみよう

A: Hi, Taichi. I'm wondering about using mizuhiki in hair and makeup when wearing *furisode*. What do you think?

B: Do you mean mizuhiki which is used for gift envelopes?

A: Yes. I like mizuhiki. It is very beautiful, so I would like to wear it.

B: Well, let me see. It looks strange to me. How about wearing a crane or turtle accessory instead?

A: Are you sure? Why? I don't wear those at all.

B: Cranes and turtles mean happiness in Japan.
I'm sure they would suit your hair and *furisode*.

4　Activity　水引の結びを英語で説明しよう

梅結び	結び切り（真結び）	あわじ結び	叶（かのう）結び
1. an ume knot	2. a kano knot	3. an Awaji knot	4. a square knot

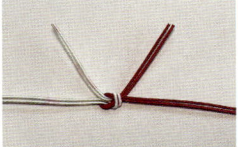   

a.	b.	c.	d.
Used for sympathy visits, Buddhist rites, and other somber occasions.	Used for weddings and celebrations. It is not easily undone so it means a long-lasting relationship.	Used for omamori, a traditional good luck charm. It means "May your wishes come true."	Used for hair accessories, decorating lunch boxes, etc.

例 （　日本語の名称　）結び in Japanese is referred to （　英語の名称　）knot in English. The picture （　絵の番号　）shows the knot of the mizuhiki. It is used for （　　用途　　）.

婚約の際に贈られる結納用品

Mizuhiki is a traditional Japanese craft that has been handed down from generation to generation.

Mizuhiki of good quality is made of strong Japanese paper. **It is not easy to weave** thin strings into shapes. Craftsmen have created many fine handmade mizuhiki, many of which were presented to athletes at the 1998 Nagano Olympics.

In recent years, however, demand for mizuhiki work has been decreasing due to fewer traditional occasions such as the *yuino,* or traditional engagement ceremony. The number of people decorating their homes with traditional mizuhiki designs, such as cranes, turtles, and pine trees, has also decreased dramatically.

Although demand for mizuhiki work for traditional uses has decreased, surprisingly, mizuhiki accessories and hair ornaments are gaining popularity, especially among young people. Many young people like earrings and hair ornaments made with Awaji knots or ume knots. **It is easy to use** them as accessories because they are reasonable. They can be made in any color, shape, or size.

Recently, we have even seen some overseas visitors wearing mizuhiki accessories. They also would be great souvenirs when traveling in Japan. You can buy them at stores, but **it is not difficult to make** simple mizuhiki accessories. Why not give it a try?

水引アクセサリー

True or false?　ペアで内容を確認しよう 💬

1. The number of people decorating their homes with mizuhiki is decreasing.
2. Only craftsmen can produce mizuhiki because **it is difficult to make.**

例 A: Is it true or false?　B: It is true, because … / It is false, because …

6 Research　水引についてもっと知ろう

水引は伝統的に祝儀袋などに使われてきましたが、最近では、手芸やハンドメイドなどでアクセサリーを作り、水引細工を始める人が増えてきています。伝統工芸としての水引は、現状では作られている場所は限られてきました。どこで作られているのでしょうか？

There are several famous mizuhiki production areas, including Nagano, Ishikawa, Kyoto, and Ehime. Iida in Nagano Prefecture produces about 70% of all mizuhiki products in Japan.

参考ウェブサイト例

飯田水引協同組合
伊予水引金封協同組合
京都結納儀式協同組合
ニッポンの手仕事図鑑

Task 1　水引が使われる機会 (occasion)、使用状況 (use)、色 (color)、形 (shape) を調べて、表 (table) にまとめてみよう

例

Occasion	Use	Color	Shape
celebration	attach to gift envelopes	gold, silver, red, white...	Awaji knot

Task 2　水引が使われる機会を1つ選んで、どのような水引が、どのように使われているかを、例のようにまとめてみよう

例

I (We) found that there are mizuhiki decorations that can be used for Christmas trees. Mizuhiki are unique and colorful and can be freely designed. And they are very beautiful, aren't they?

水引アクセサリーは簡単に作れます。作り方の動画などを調べながら好きな色の水引アクセサリーやキーホルダーを作ってみよう。

kano knot

Awaji knot

ume knot

How to make mizuhiki:

1. Decide which type you want to make, a kano knot, an Awaji knot or an ume knot.
2. Choose two or three colors of mizuhiki.
3. Gather the strings together and slowly weave them together.
4. If they become tangled, stop weaving and straighten them.
5. **It is important not to pull** them too hard.
6. Once you have finished weaving, flatten the design, and then you are finished.

用意するもの：水引、ピン、接着剤など

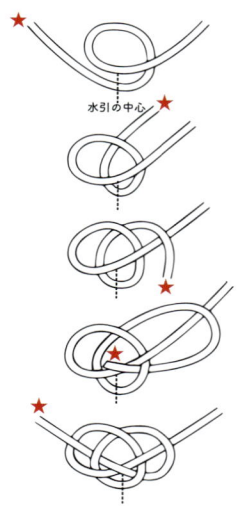
Awaji knot

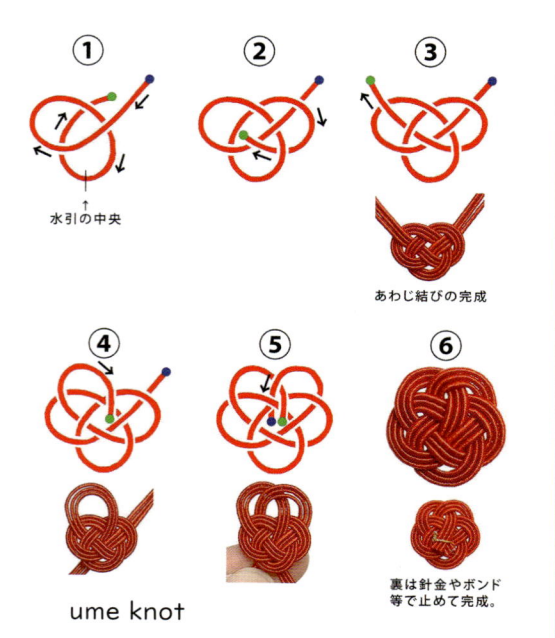
ume knot

加賀水引　津田 https://mizuhiki.jp/mizuhikiasobi/

Presentation　自分が作った水引について発表しよう

Hello everyone. We are Group 1. I'm Kanako. Today, we'd like to talk about the mizuhiki key chain we made. **It was fun to make** an ume knot. It turned out nicely. I would like to put it on my bag. We were surprised at how easy it was. Thank you for listening.

Presentation Phrase Building 6

- It turned out nicely. 　　　　うまく仕上がりました。
- I was surprised at how easy it was. 　意外と簡単で驚きました。
- It was fun to make an ume knot. 　梅結びを作るのは楽しかったです。

プレゼンテーションの原稿を書いてみよう

Reflection: Self-assessment (A = 100 – 70% B = 69 – 40% C = 39 – 0%)

Content			Language		
A	B	C	A	B	C

Reflect on your learning in English.　英語でふりかえりをまとめよう

Travelogue in Japan　にほん伝統工芸紀行③

Satsuma kiriko is characterized by its blurred cut.
薩摩切子はぼかしたカットが特徴です。

There are many good children's toys in Kumamoto.
熊本には、子どもの玩具がたくさんあります。

薩摩切子

キーホルダー作り

九州は多くの伝統工芸品で知られています。たとえば、鹿児島には「薩摩切子」というガラス細工があります。金属製の回転砥石を研磨剤と一緒にガラスに押しつけて研磨したり、溝を入れたりしてデザインを施していきます。島津藩の別邸だった仙巌園では薩摩切子の製作体験をすることができます。輝く色がとても美しいガラスを組み合わせ、レジンという液体を使って加工すると、写真のような薩摩切子のキーホルダーができました。

鹿児島には現在も噴火活動が続く桜島があります。火山灰に覆われた桜島では、「桜島溶岩焼き」と呼ばれる工芸品があります。釉薬に桜島の火山灰を利用した陶芸作品のことで、鉄分を多く含んだ光沢のある作品になります。写真は桜島溶岩焼きのコーヒーカップです。

桜島溶岩焼きカップ

肥後の変り独楽

肥後コマ © トップクラフト

肥後コマはインドネシアや中国から伝わり、江戸時代から子どもたちの遊びに欠かせない玩具です。肥後コマには種類があり、形に合わせて「デベソ」「マンジュウ」といった名前がついています。

Japanese Traditional Crafts

Task   What craft are you interested in? Share ideas with your classmates.

因習和紙
© 伝統工芸 青山スクエア

Inshu-washi is Japanese paper manufactured in Tottori. It is often used for calligraphy and ink painting. *Inshu-washi* making has continued since the Heian period. This *washi* paper was used by common people during the Edo period. It was the first *washi* paper in Japan to be designated as a national traditional craft.

熊野筆

Kumano brushes are made in Kumano, Hiroshima. They are made of animal hair from deer, wild boar, and other animals. While they are famous for calligraphy, recently they have become popular as cosmetic brushes and are used by professional makeup artists.

ビードロ

Poppen is hand-blown glass, or vidro, from Nagasaki. Molten glass is attached to the end of a long pipe, and a round shape is created by carefully blowing a bubble. It was introduced from Portugal during the Edo period. *Poppen* is a famous glass toy that makes a 'pecompekong' sound when blown.

キジ馬

Kijiuma from the Hitoyoshi region of Kumamoto, is a colorful toy developed in the Heian period. On the forehead of the *kijiuma* is written "大," but the reason for this is still a mystery. They range from tiny ones to ones big enough for a child to ride on.

花手箱

Hanatebako is another local toy from the Hitoyoshi region. It is said that a samurai from the Heike clan who came from Kyoto during the Heian period made it while thinking of the gorgeous city of Kyoto. The box is made of wood, and decorated with painted red and white camellia flowers.

八重山ミンサー織

Minsa, from the Yaeyama region of Okinawa, is woven from cotton yarn. "*Min*" means cotton and "*Sa*" means belt. It was given by a woman to a man as a wedding gift in the old days. It is woven with patterns of four and five squares, meaning *itsuno* (five) and *yomademo* (four).

Lesson 7 Japanese Curry
カレー

🔊 29 日本の「カレー」は、日本食ということを知っていますか？

Do you like curry? Curry is a very popular dish. There are many different versions of curry around the world, and it is made with a variety of ingredients and spices. Did you know that Japanese curry is different from other Asian curries? We often call it *curry rice*. It is important **to know** a lot more about Japanese curry.

1 Warmup talk　英語で話してみよう

例　A: What kind of curry do you like?
　　B: I like chicken curry. I especially love curry with chicken wings.

🔊 30 2 Keywords　英語でどう言えばいいの？

漢方薬	I want to take *kampo* **medicine** that doesn't have side effects.
薬の効能	It is necessary for supplements to have proven **health benefits**.
材料、食材	Miso soup has a variety of **ingredients** such as tofu and vegetables.
料理	I like Turkish **cuisine**, such as donerkebab and baklaba.
和食	*Washoku* includes sushi, miso soup, and Japanese local dishes.
カレー粉	There are many different types of **curry powder** at this shop.
薬膳	Enjoy medicinal cuisine such as *yakuzen* pot or curry.
カレールー	Many types of Japanese **curry roux** are very convenient.
コンビニ	**Convenience stores** are very popular in Asian countries.
レトルトカレー	Supermarkets in Japan sell many varieties of **packaged curry**.

3 **Dialogue**　役割を決めてやってみよう

A: Do you have curry for lunch? Did you make it yourself? It smells really exotic, doesn't it?

B: Yes. I like **to cook and eat**. I mix the spices myself **to make** curry.

A: Really? Great. I believe curry can cure a cold. Did you put apples and honey in it?

B: I agree with you, but I don't want to have apples or honey in my curry. Spices have benefits.

A: What do you mean?

B: Do you know that spices have health benefits?
Spices have actually been used in medicine.

A: They are certainly used in Chinese or *kampo* medicine.

B: For example, ginger and garlic are good **to warm** up the body. That's why I like to eat curry.

A: Is it possible **to try** a little bit of your curry?

B: No!

4 **Activity**　カレーのスパイスを知ろう

カレーにはスパイス（香辛料）が入っています。英語でなんと言うのか、どのような効能 (health benefits) があるか、話し合ってみよう。

鬱金（うこん）	陳皮（ちんぴ）	黒胡椒
茴香（ういきょう）	馬芹（うまぜり）	丁子（ちょうじ）
八角（はっかく）	肉桂（にっけい）	肉荳（にくずく）

mandarin	star anise	nutmeg
turmeric	black pepper	cloves
cumin	fennel	cinnamon

 A: What is the English word for 鬱金？
　　B: It is turmeric. Turmeric can be good for diarrhea.

Curry is a popular Indian cuisine which describes a sauce flavored with a variety of spices: including ginger, garlic, fennel, mace, cumin, coriander, cardamom, cinnamon and turmeric. When a person travels globally, Indian restaurants are found easily. Curry makes use of local ingredients and influences **to create** unique dishes all over the world.

Historically, during the 17th century when England ruled India, curry was introduced to Europe and adapted into a European-style stew. By the late 18th century, curry powder emerged, and curry dishes became briefly popular in European countries. Curry came to Japan in the early Meiji period from England along with its cooking method, quickly spreading as curry and rice. Curry is now popular and is eaten at home and in restaurants. Curry is usually served with rice, so Japanese people call it *curry rice*, but there are many different curry dishes people can enjoy eating.

Curry uses many spices that also belong to traditional Chinese herbal medicine. It is called *kampo* medicine in Japan. We have a cuisine called *yakuzen* or medicinal cooking that has been created based on *kampo* medicine. These days some people like **to eat** *yakuzen* curry, which contains ingredients that make you healthy.

Japanese curry made with lots of spices is now a part of *washoku*. Its popularity extends to Japanese homes and tourists from other countries. In addition, there are lots of instant curry roux and packaged curry products at supermarkets and convenience stores. There are also a growing number of curry restaurants in urban areas.

True or false?   ペアで内容を確認しよう

1. Curry didn't originate in Japan, but it has developed in its own unique way.
2. Japanese curry is very popular and healthy, and it is now eaten all over the world.

例 A: Is it true or false?   B: It's true, because … / It's false, because …

6 Research　カレーのスパイスについてもっと知ろう

カレーはたくさんのスパイスを混ぜて作ります。代表的なスパイスの効能や原産地をインターネットなどで調べてみましょう。

There are hundreds of spices around the world. Spices have health benefits. Curry ingredients include:

cumin	coriander	cardamom	cinnamon	turmeric
クミン	コリアンダー	カルダモン	シナモン	ターメリック

Task 1　それぞれのスパイスの効能と原産地を表にまとめてみよう

Name	Health benefits	Origin
例 cumin	It promotes digestion, reduces food-borne infections, promotes weight loss, improves blood sugar and cholesterol levels.	Egypt and the Middle East
coriander		
cardamom		
cinnamon		
turmeric		

Task 2　他にも興味のあるスパイスについて調べて特徴をまとめ話してみよう

chili	black pepper	fenugreek	ginger	garlic	fennel	caraway
clove	mustard	nutmeg	thyme	sage	cayenne	marjoram

例

ginger

I like ginger. Ginger is one of the most widely known spices in the world. Ginger tea is good for a cold or a sore throat. My grandmother always made ginger tea when I had a cold or a sore throat. She said ginger has a warming effect. It is easy to make ginger tea. You first add grated ginger to hot water with lemon and drink it. Give it a try.

自分や友達、家族など周りの人たちの体の不調をインタビューして、その不調の回復のためのスパイスを組み合わせた薬膳カレー (*yakuzen* curry) のレシピを考えましょう。ポイントは食材です。薬膳食材 (*yakuzen* ingredients) で調べて、食材を工夫してください。

How to cook *yakuzen* curry:

Ingredients: meat, onions, potatoes, carrots, vegetable oil, water, spices, garlic, ginger

Method:

1. Prepare meat, vegetables, and spices that have health benefits.
2. First add garlic, ginger and spices to the meat and sauteé until it browns. Then remove from pot.
3. Fry the onions in a large pot until they change color.
4. Return the browned meat to the pot and add chopped carrots, potatoes, and water. Bring to a gentle boil.
5. Simmer while stirring occasionally until the vegetables are softened.

My *Yakuzen* Curry Recipe

Ingredients:
Method: ①   ②   ③

Hi, I'm Ken. I have made my favorite *yakuzen* curry recipe. Do you like curry rice? I love all types of curry. Indian curry, Japanese curry, and soup curry. I especially like cup curry noodles. They are very convenient. It is okay to add some spices. I would like to have beautiful skin. I hear cinnamon can help produce collagen and might help my skin look younger. Please give it a try.

Presentation Phrase Building 7

- It is very convenient.　　　それはとても便利です。
- It is okay to add some spices.　スパイスを入れてもいいでしょう。
- Please give it a try.　　　　ぜひ試してみてください。

プレゼンテーションの原稿を書いてみよう

Reflection: Self-assessment (A = 100 – 70% B = 69 – 40% C = 39 – 0%)

Content			Language		
A	B	C	A	B	C

Reflect on your learning in English.　英語でふりかえりをまとめよう

Lesson 8 Karate
空手

🔊 33 **空手にはどんな動きがあるのでしょうか？**

Japan is famous for its martial arts, and karate is one of the most popular. There are karate dojos all over the world, even as far away as Iceland! **Have** you ever practiced Karate? Even if you **haven't** learned karate yourself, you **have** probably seen people doing it. It is known for simple but effective punches, blocks, and kicks. Karate-*ka* spend years, in many cases decades, perfecting their techniques. But how and where did this famous Japanese martial art develop?

---

1 Warmup talk　英語で話してみよう

例　A: What kind of moves are in karate?
　　B: I think there are kicks and punches.

🔊 34 ## 2 Keywords　英語でどう言えばいいの？

〜について調べる	I'm **reading up on** the national karate team members who were at the Tokyo Olympics.
〜と関係がある	I think karate **has something to do with** martial arts.
それは聞いたことがある気がする	You're right! **That rings a bell**.
〜に移住する	Many people **emigrate to** countries that have more job opportunities.
行ってみるかな！	**Maybe I'll check it out** next time I'm there.
攻撃と防御のテクニック	Karate has both **offensive and defensive techniques**.
蹴り、突き、受け	Karate has many kinds of **kicks**, **strikes**, and **blocks**.
道場訓	We recite the **dojo-kun**, the guiding principles for karate-*ka*, before each training.

3 Dialogue　役割を決めてやってみよう

A: Hi, Jenny! What are you up to?

B: Hi, Scott! I'm just looking online at information for this year's Nisei Week.

A: Nisei Week? What's that?

B: **I've** been reading up on it. The history is really interesting!

A: If it's called Nisei Week, **could** it have something to do with Japanese roots?

B: Yes! That's right! Many Japanese people emigrated to the United States in the late 1800's and early 1900's. They were called "Issei," or first generation. Their children were called "Nisei," or second generation.

A: Yes! That rings a bell!

B: Apparently in 1934, Nisei living in Los Angeles developed a summer festival to celebrate Japanese and Japanese-American culture and arts. It's held every year.

A: Sounds fantastic! Maybe **I'll** check it out this year!

B: You **should**! Last year I saw flower arranging, judo, karate, and dance demonstrations.

A: Karate too? I'm definitely going this year!

4 Activity　空手の技を知ろう

次の技の名前がどの絵か話し合ってみよう。

a) downward block　b) front kick　　c) outside block　d) reverse front punch
e) back kick　　　　f) front lunge punch　g) side kick　　h) upward block

① 　② 　③ 　④

⑤ 　⑥ 　⑦ 　⑧

例 A: Which illustration shows downward block?

B: I think it is illustration 5.

A: Can we use it as an offensive or defensive technique?

B: I think we can use it as a defensive technique.

Karate is a widely practiced martial art with a rich history. It combines elements of traditional Japanese and Okinawan fighting styles. The development of modern karate **can** be traced back to the early 20th century.

The roots of karate **can** be found in Okinawa. Okinawan martial arts were influenced by Chinese martial arts and indigenous fighting techniques. Trade and cultural exchanges, particularly during the 17th to 19th centuries between Okinawa and various regions of China led to this transfer of martial arts knowledge. Techniques such as kicks, strikes, and blocks as well as forms (*kata*) were among the elements adopted from Chinese systems.

The indigenous fighting styles of Okinawa were referred to as *Te* and *Tode* before they became known as karate. Historically, the people of Okinawa were not permitted to have weapons. Because of this, Okinawans developed methods of self-defense that focused on unarmed combat. Techniques were adapted which led to the development of karate, which literally means "empty hand."

Gichin Funakoshi is widely acknowledged to be the father of modern karate. Born in Shuri, Okinawa, in 1868, he is often credited with introducing karate to mainland Japan.

In 1922, Funakoshi gave a demonstration in Tokyo, and received a positive response. He decided to stay in Tokyo and open his first dojo named the Shotokan. Funakoshi's teachings focused not only on the physical techniques of karate but also on its philosophical aspects, such as the development of character, self-discipline, and respect.

Karate's practicality, philosophy, and emphasis on self-defense appeal to people worldwide. Today, modern karate **has** evolved into a diverse and global martial art practiced by millions of individuals across the world.

True or false?　ペアで内容を確認しよう

1. People outside of Japan are not interested in karate.
2. Traditional Okinawan fighting styles involve the use of weapons.

例 A: Is it true or false?　B: It's true, because … / It's fales, because …

6 Research　Nisei Week という祭りについて知ろう

日本の文化は外国でどのように紹介されているのでしょうか？アメリカ・ロサンゼルスのリトルトーキョーで開かれている Nisei Week はどのような祭りなのか調べてみましょう。

Task 1　Nisei Week の情報をまとめてみよう

Nisei Week の情報を検索しましょう。まず英語のウェブサイトを見て、日本語版は確認のツールとして利用しましょう。

Where on the website?	What kind of information?
例 community section	We can find information about Nisei Week sponsors.

Task 2　次の2つの質問についてグループで話し合おう

a) Do you think it is easy to find information on this website? Give reasons for your answer.

b) How could this website be improved?

道場訓とは、空手家が道場の内外で守るべき5つの指針のことです。海外でも道場訓を暗唱している道場があります。

Let's write our own copy of the dojo-*kun* in English.

The dojo-*kun* is a set of five guiding principles that karate-*ka* are expected to follow both in and out of the dojo. They are considered fundamental to the practice of karate. It is typically recited at the beginning of a training session to remind students of their commitment to these values. Dojos outside of Japan also recite the dojo-*kun*. Some recite a translated version, while others memorize and recite the original Japanese version.

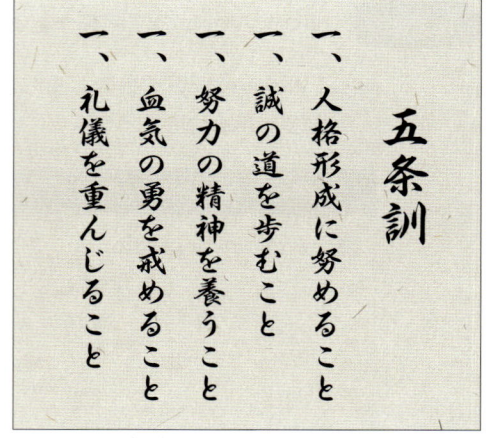

The dojo-*kun* written in Japanese calligraphy

How to write the dojo-*kun*:

1. Prepare the paper (use the worksheet) and pens that you would like to use.
2. Make a rough draft of the dojo-*kun* with pencil.
3. Trace the words with the pen that you chose.

用意するもの：紙（ワークシート）、鉛筆、黒のマーカーペンまたは筆ペン

The following is the dojo-*kun* in both English and Japanese. It must be written in the order it appears. But, because each principle is equally important, do not number them.

The dojo-*kun*	
Japanese	**English**
一つ、人格形成に努めること。	Seek perfection of character.
一つ、誠の道を守ること。	Follow the path of sincerity.
一つ、努力の精神を養うこと。	Put maximum effort into everything you do.
一つ、礼儀を重んずること。	Respect others.
一つ、血気の勇を戒むること。	Develop self-control.

Hello everyone! My name is Nora. I am going to talk about my favorite dojo-*kun* principle. I like the fourth one, "respect others." I like it because I think that by respecting others, we can end bullying in schools. Thank you for listening!

Presentation Phrase Building 8

- My favourite dojo-*kun* principle is ～.　私のお気に入りの道場訓は～
- I like it because I think that ～.　好きな理由は～だからです。
- By (respecting others) we **can** (end bullying).
  （相手を尊重する）ことで、（いじめをなくす）ことができます。

プレゼンテーションの原稿を書いてみよう

Reflection: Self-assessment (A = 100 – 70% B = 69 – 40% C = 39 – 0%)

Content			Language		
A	B	C	A	B	C

Reflect on your learning in English.　英語でふりかえりをまとめよう

Travelogue in Japan　にほん伝統工芸紀行④

In Japan, it is said that no part of a whale is wasted.

日本では、鯨には捨てるところはないと言われています。

There are handicrafts made from their whiskers and bones.

ヒゲや骨を使った工芸品があります。

和歌山県太地町（たいじ）は昔から「古式捕鯨」発祥の地として有名です。その歴史は古く、江戸時代から始まりました。住人の苗字には捕鯨と関連したものも見られます。現在は商業捕鯨が禁止され、昔のように捕鯨は行われていませんが、町民の生活は鯨と共にあり、鯨の供養碑や、かつて鯨を見張ったり狼煙をあげていた場所などもあります。

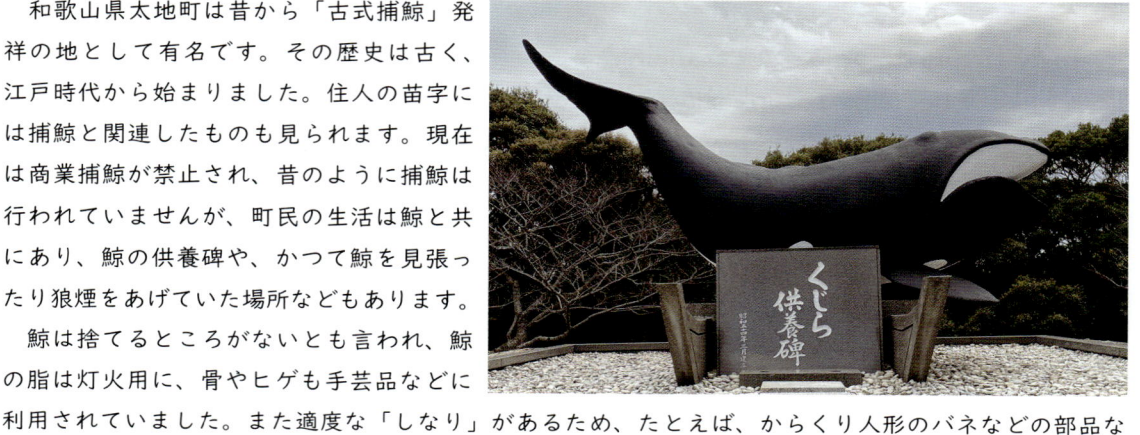

鯨は捨てるところがないとも言われ、鯨の脂は灯火用に、骨やヒゲも手芸品などに利用されていました。また適度な「しなり」があるため、たとえば、からくり人形のバネなどの部品などに使用されていました。また、歯は印鑑などにも加工されています。龍涎香（りゅうぜんこう）とよばれる香料は、マッコウクジラの腸内に発生する結石を原料としています。

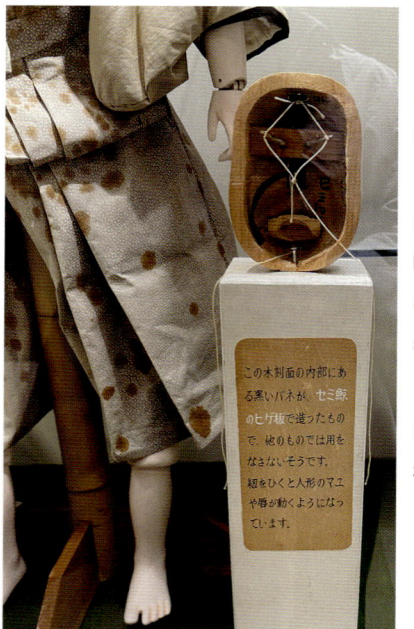

この木刻面の内部にある黒いバネは、セミ鯨のヒゲ板で造ったもので、他のものでは用をなさないそうです。綱をひくと人形のマユや唇が動くようになっています。

しかし、鯨を獲らなくなっただけではなく、加工に手間暇がかかったり、職人の高齢化や、プラスティックなどの代替品もできたため、鯨を加工する技術は失われていっています。

鯨が地域住民の生活に密着していたので、鯨車や勢子舟（捕鯨用漁船）などの、鯨を模したおもちゃ（民芸品）もあります。これらは捕鯨が盛んであった高知県や長崎県にもあります。

Japanese Traditional Crafts

Task What craft are you interested in? Share ideas with your classmates.

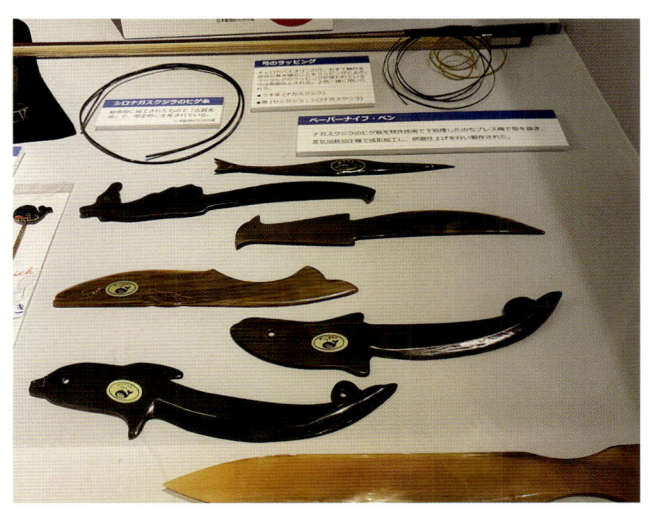

Whalebone: The beautiful yellow–white baleen of the sperm whale, known for its suitable flexibility, was highly valued. It was used for items like hairpins, tea coasters, dessert plates, and – because of its flexibility – for fishing rods, ear cleaners, backscratchers (magonote), and shoehorns.

There is also a local toy called "whale ship," although it is not made from actual whales. It's said that fishermen who were away fishing made these as souvenirs for their children waiting at home.

Lesson 9 Fermented Food
発酵食品

🔊 38 **多くの発酵食品があります。発酵のしくみを知っていますか？**

Do you like *natto*, *tsukemono*, or *katsuobushi*? They are fermented foods which we call 発酵食品 (*hakko shokuhin*) in Japanese. These foods are very healthy. What is fermented food? Or what is the process of fermentation? Fermentation is a chemical process **which** is caused by microorganisms: molds, yeasts, and bacteria.

1 Warmup talk 英語で話してみよう

例 A: I eat *natto* rice every morning. I like it very much.

B: Really? I like to have cheese and yogurt for my breakfast.

🔊 39 2 Keywords 英語でどう言えばいいの？

発酵	Carbon dioxide is produced by yeast during **fermentation**.
菌、カビ	You can find **mold** almost anywhere.
酵母、イースト	**Yeasts** are used in baking and making alcoholic beverages.
こうじ	There are over 100 different ***koji*** molds in Japan.
細菌	**Bacteria** are able to live in a wide variety of environments.
乳酸菌 (LAB)	Yogurt is a healthy food produced from **lactic acid bacteria**.
酢酸菌 (AAB)	Vinegar is a food product made by **acetic acid bacteria**.
納豆菌	*Natto* is a soybean product fermented by ***natto* bacteria**.
発酵食品	**Fermented foods** include wine, beer, cheese, and chocolate.
食塩水	**Brine** is a solution of salt and water used for preserving.

3 Dialogue　役割を決めてやってみよう

A: Good morning, Shun. Thank you for coming to the airport yesterday.

B: Morning, Cathy. It's our pleasure. We hope you will enjoy traveling in Japan.

A: Your family are all very kind. Thanks a lot. Are you eating Japanese breakfast?

B: Yes, I'm eating rice, miso soup, fried eggs, and *natto*.

A: Ah, *natto*! I hear it smells awful but tastes good. Please tell me how to eat it.

B: It's easy. I'll show you. You just mix it, add soy sauce, and eat it with rice.

A: Okay. I'll try it. … It smells bad, but it's good. Oishii!

B: Sure. *Natto* is a fermented food made from soybeans. It's healthy.

A: I am very interested in fermented food in Japan. Please let me know.

B: Would you like to try other Japanese foods such as *umeboshi*, *tsukemono*, or *katsuobushi*?

4 Activity　発酵に必要な微生物について知ろう

発酵食品 (fermented food) がどの微生物 (microorganism) の働きによって生まれるのか、調べて話し合ってみよう。

shoyu / soy sauce	*su* / vinegar	sake	miso
kimuchi	*mirin*	bread	yogurt
wine	beer	*natto*	*shochu*
tsukemono / pickles	cheese	*kanzuri*	

koji molds　こうじ菌　_____

yeasts　酵母　_____

lactic acid bacteria　乳酸菌　_____

acetic acid bacteria　酢酸菌　_____

natto bacteria　納豆菌　_____

Fermentation is the chemical process in **which** microorganisms bring about changes in food and have beneficial effects on our health. Fermented food not only enhances taste, nutritional value, and shelf life, but also improves gut health and antioxidant levels.

You can find mold almost anywhere there is moisture and oxygen. It belongs to the fungi kingdom and lives in moist places. *Koji* mold grows and ferments on the surface of rice. Yeast is also fungi. There are many kinds of yeast. Though some yeast types are harmful to us, most are very useful, for example, in making bread and drinks. Yeast grows well anywhere **that** sugar is found. Bacteria is also found all over, such as in soil, on rocks, and in seas and oceans. Some bacteria live in or on plants and animals. Your body houses bacteria as well.

Koji mold called aspergillus oryzae is used for *sake* brewing. During the fermentation process, aspergillus oryzae produces enzymes that turn rice starch into glucose, then yeast turns the glucose into alcohol. *Koji* mold releases amino acids **that** add *umami*.

Yeast is used in the production of bread, cake, and wine. It can ferment sugar to produce ethanol and carbon dioxide, **which** makes bread and cake soft and fluffy. *Natto* bacteria found in soil is used to ferment soybeans and make them sticky. The stickiness can lower blood sugar levels. Lactic acid bacteria (LAB) and acetic acid bacteria (AAB) play important roles in various fermented foods. For example, LAB can help regulate digestion and AAB can lower blood pressure and inflammation.

True or false?　ペアで内容を確認しよう

1. Mold, yeast, and bacteria are all useful for creating healthy fermented foods.

2. *Koji* mold, yeast, *natto* bacteria, LAB, and AAB are essential for *sake* brewing.

例 A: Is it true or false?　B: It's true, because … / It's false, because …

6   Research   世界の発酵食品を調べよう

発酵食品 (fermented food) は日本だけではなく、古くから世界中にたくさんあります。よく知られているものは、ヨーグルト (yogurt)、チーズ (cheese)、ワイン (wine) などです。日本も含めてどのような発酵食品があるのか調べてみましょう。

例   sauerkraut   surströmming   fonofe   kiviak   tempeh   kvass

Task 1   例の世界の発酵食品 (fermented food) について調べて表にまとめてみよう

Name	Features	Country
surströmming	It is a type of pickled herring fermented in salt inside a can.	Sweden

Task 2   1つ選んで詳しく調べてまとめ、互いに共有しよう

例   Surströmming is a very famous fermented canned food in Sweden. This fermented food is notorious for being one of the smelliest foods in the world. Some people say, "It smells like a dead body." I have never experienced such a rotten smell. This canned food includes herring, **which** are called *nishin* in Japanese.

The smell is unbearable, but some say, "It tastes quite nice." I want to give it a try. The fermentation process is simple. First, herring are soaked in a barrel of brine or salty water, and then they are canned.

実際に発酵を体験してみましょう。食品の発酵はもちろんですが、発酵の利用は食品だけではありません。発酵の例を紹介します。実際にやってみて、英語でレポートを作成しましょう。

参考 1

How to ferment vegetables （野菜の発酵（浅漬け）のしかた）:

❶ Start with a jar. Wash it with warm water and dry it well. Next, place it in the boilig water for 15 minutes.

❷ Prepare vegetables. Wash them and slice, dice, shred or grate them. Add some tiny onions.

❸ Make a brine by mixing salt into water. The amount of salt depends on your personal preference.

❹ Add the vegetables, arranging them in the jar.

❺ Pour the brine over the vegetables, making sure they are covered. Press down gently to remove any air bubbles and screw the lid on tight.

❻ Leave it to ferment at room temperature for around three days.

❼ When the vegetables start to bubble and develop a sour scent, move them to the fridge. Leave them to ferment for a week before eating.

藍を発酵させて染める液を「藍建て (indigo vat)」（①藍 (indigo)、②還元剤 (reducing agent)、③灰（水酸化カルシウム (a base) などを使用して作成）といいます。発酵は藍染めにも利用されています。インターネットなどで調べてみましょう。
布や糸 (cloth or yarn) を染める手順の基本は次のとおりです。

参考 2

How to dye with indigo （藍染めの手順）:

❶ Scrub the cloth or yarn.

❷ Build a vat for dyeing.

❸ Dip the cloth or yarn.

❹ Oxidize the cloth or yarn.

❺ Do a final wash of the cloth or yarn.

Hello, everyone! Today, I'd like to talk about the wonders of fermentation. When it comes to fermentation, we immediately think of food, but there are also other things that use fermentation. Do you know about indigo dyeing or 藍染め？ Fermentation is used for this. I bought an indigo dyeing kit online. It's very easy to experience indigo dyeing this way. This is my indigo dyed cloth. It is beautiful. I hope you will also do indigo dyeing. Thank you for your attention.

Presentation Phrase Building 9

- I'd like to talk about the wonders ～ .　　～の不思議について話したい。
- I hope you will also do ～ .　　あなたたちが～をしてみることを願います。

プレゼンテーションの原稿を書いてみよう

Reflection: Self-assessment (A = 100 – 70% B = 69 – 40% C = 39 – 0%)

Content			Language		
A	B	C	A	B	C

Reflect on your learning in English.　英語でふりかえりをまとめよう

Lesson 10 Mallorca Tiles
マジョリカタイル

🔊 42 **マジョリカタイルを見たことがありますか？**

Mallorca originally referred to wares made **in Mediterranean Europe** and primarily exported through the port of Mallorca **in Spain**. However, in the Taisho period, Mallorca tiles were made **in Japan** and exported to the world. You can still see Japan-made Mallorca tiles **in many countries** now.

1 Warmup talk　英語で話してみよう

例　A: Why were Japan-made Mallorca tiles exported to the world?
　　B: Spain and Japan collaborated to make them, I think.

🔊 43 2 Keywords　英語でどう言えばいいの？

マジョリカタイル	You can see Japan-made **Mallorca tiles** in Kyoto.
（陶器などの）製品	Kutani **ware** is famous for its bright colors.
改修する	That hotel has **renovated** the reception floor.
公衆浴場、銭湯	**Public bathhouses** have been popular in Japan.
対称的な図案	Most Mallorca tiles have **symmetrical designs**.
レリーフ	This tile is one of the most beautiful **reliefs** in Japan.
陶器、土器	**Pottery** is opaque, but porcelain is translucent.
釉薬	Ceramic **glaze** is a coating for decoration and design.
焼き物を焼く	I would like to **fire** ceramic tiles in Spain.
窯	**Kilns** are an essential part of pottery manufacture.

Dialogue　役割を決めてやってみよう

A: Hi, Lucas. Do you want to get some coffee?

B: Oh, hi, Tak. Sure. I know a good café **in Kyoto.**

A: What kind of café?

B: It is an antique café with high ceilings and walls. They are covered entirely with Japan-made Mallorca tiles.

A: Sorry, what is a Mallorca tile?

B: Look at this photo. The café is renovated from an 80-year-old public bathhouse. Here are some of the designs.

A: Mallorca tiles are beautiful, aren't they? Let me see, I've seen those tiles, which are **in my grandma's bathroom and kitchen.**

B: Good. Why don't you renovate your grandma's house and turn it into a café?

Café SARASA

4　Activity　マジョリカタイルの模様を知ろう

次のマジョリカタイルの模様 (pattern) は英語でどのように言うのか、話し合ってみよう。

Mallorca tiles often use symmetrical patterns.

A: No.1 is 長方形. What is this shape in English?

B: Maybe it's a rectangle.

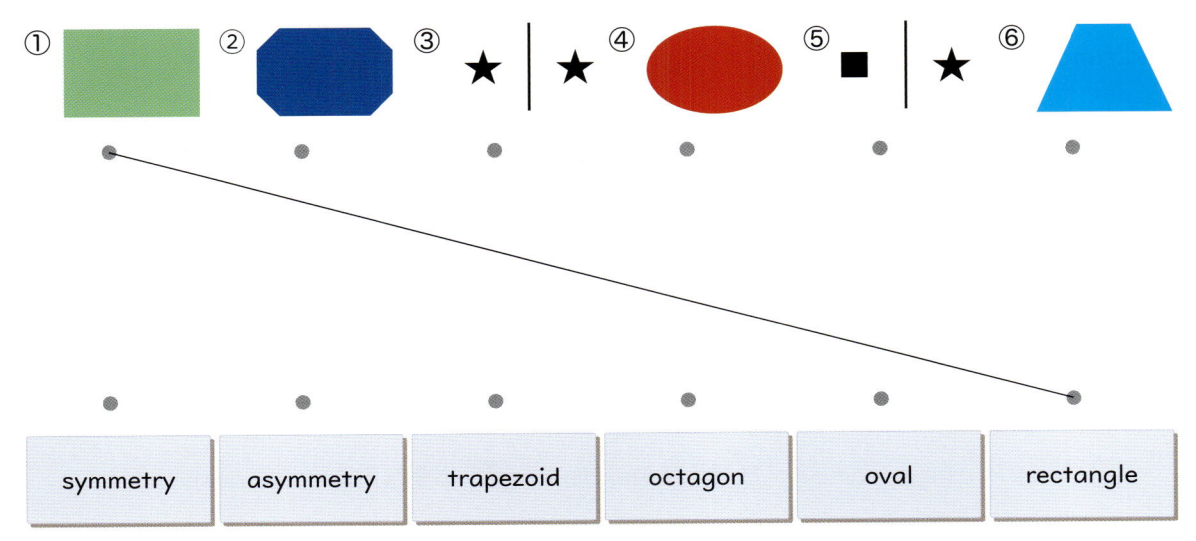

| symmetry | asymmetry | trapezoid | octagon | oval | rectangle |

Japan-made Mallorca tiles are colorful reliefs. They were exported to the world in the Taisho and Showa periods. As a matter of fact, these tiles were created **in Japan** by imitating the Victorian tiles of England. Tile makers **in England** named them Mallorca tiles to reflect their roots, because they were influenced by Mallorca pottery from Spain. Japan-made Mallorca tiles also have this name.

Old tile (Spain)

You still can see Japan-made Mallorca tiles used **in many countries.** For example, if you travel to Zanzibar, which is located **in the Indian Ocean** 15 miles off the coast of Tanzania **in Africa,** you'll find Japan-made Mallorca tiles **in the tomb** of the Queen of Zanzibar. And if you visit Taiwan, you can see many of them **in restaurants or hotels.**

Cuerda-Seca

Mallorca pottery has specific techniques. One characteristic is that glaze is applied as a base before painting. In the Cuenca technique, a mold is pressed into a clay slab to create an outline of the design. The Cuerda-Seca technique involves designing with oil-based pigment, pouring glaze over the design, and repelling the oil off.

Today, ceramic tiles are becoming popular, because they are attractive and don't break easily. Japan-made Mallorca tiles are especially easy to clean and do spot repairs on. These tiles are used as retro design tools **in cafés, hotels, and restaurants.** They can be used to divide larger open spaces into different sections and functions.

True or false?　ペアで内容を確認しよう

1. Cuenca involves designing with oil-based pigment, and pouring glaze over the design.

2. In the Taisho and Showa periods, Japan-made Mallorca tiles were exported all over the world.

例 A: Is it true or false?　B: It's true, because … / It's false, because …

6 Research マジョリカタイルについてもっと知ろう

マジョリカタイルはスペインが発祥ですが、タイルの歴史を見ると、エジプトには世界最古のタイルが存在します。その歴史を調べてみましょう。

The oldest tile in the world is a rectangular tile, which is 62mm long and 38mm wide with a blue-green glaze. It is 4,650 years old. It was found in the basement of an Egyptian pyramid. Going back in history, these tiles may have been used since the time civilization arose on Earth.

INAX ライブミュージアム蔵

Task 1 タイルについて調べてみよう

Name	Characteristics or techniques	Where you see
Cuenca	cream to buff in color, off-white background, painted in blue, green, manganese, honey, or gold, with geometric design motifs	Alhambra Palace (Granada, Spain)

mosaic tile

marble tile

metal tile

Task 2 マジョリカタイルを使った建物を1つ選び、詳しく調べてみよう

例 Retro tiles can also be seen at the Mallorca tile museum in Taiwan. Mallorca tiles were not only used to decorate house entrances and roofs, but also for interior decoration.

台湾花磚博物館

写真提供：中園まりえ

マジョリカタイルのデザインをヒントにして、デザインの模様を考えて実際に紙に描いてみよう。
特徴は、幾何学模様とシンメトリーと色です。

実際に楽やき (raku firing) をしてみましょう。10cm サイズのセラミックタイル
(ceramic fiber board) を使って簡単に作成できます。カラーペンで図柄を描いた
タイルをオーブンで焼くと色落ちせず、コースターとして使用できます。

参考　らくやきマーカー（エポックコミカル）、PORCELAINE marker（Pebeo）
　　　などが市販されています。

実際にセラミックタイル（10cm サイズ）を作成する手順です。

How to make an original Mallorca tile:

❶ Imagine a tile design. Think of a pattern that is as symmetrical as possible.

❷ Remove oil, dirt, etc. from the ceramic fiber board.

❸ Draw a rough sketch on the ceramic fiber board.

❹ Paint the ceramic fiber board starting from the lightest color.

❺ Paint over it to make the color darker.

❻ Place it in the kiln and fire it at about 200°C for 20 to 30 minutes.

❼ Cool it for about an hour after firing, and then rinse it with water.

Hello everyone. I am Ayaka. Today I would like to talk about my Mallorca-like tile or its design idea. I have a black cat. We have lived together for a long time. So, I designed cat eyes and whiskers. I chose yellow, black and orange. Because she has yellow eyes. I tried to make it symmetrical. Thank you for listening.

Presentation Phrase Building 10

- I have a black cat.　　私は黒い猫を飼っています。
- I designed it to be symmetrical.　　対称になるようにデザインしました。
- Because she has yellow eyes.　　なぜなら彼女は黄色い目をしているからです。

プレゼンテーションの原稿を書いてみよう

Reflection: Self-assessment (A = 100 – 70%　B = 69 – 40%　C = 39 – 0%)

Content	Language
A　　B　　C	A　　B　　C

Reflect on your learning in English.　英語でふりかえりをまとめよう

Picture Candles

No. _____ Name _____

My Picture Candle

Choose your flowers and design your picture candle.

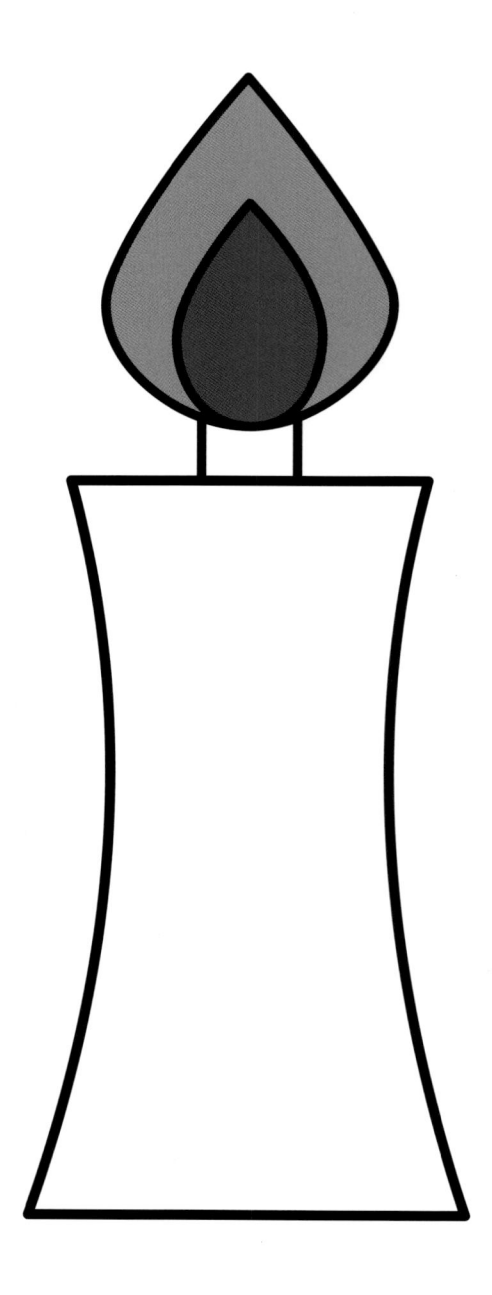

The Furoshiki

No. _____ Name _____

Wrapping with Furoshiki

Think about how to wrap items with *furoshiki* and present your ideas to the class.

Title: 2 bottle wrapping		
	Wrapping procedures	Illustrations photo
①	This is a method for wrapping two bottles or one-shō bottles (approximately 1.8 liters). It's best to adjust the size of the *furoshiki* to the size of the bottles.	
②		
③		

Travelogue in Japan ①

No. _____ Name _____

Write a brief travel guide about Japanese traditional crafts from Hokkaido, Tohoku, and Kanto.

| Name of the traditional craft: |

_____

| Illustration or photo: |

Travel guide:

_____

_____

_____

_____

_____

_____

The Namahage

No. _____   Name _____

My Namahage Mask

Design your Namahage mask by adding materials, colors, and details.

The Sanshin

No. _____ Name _____

My *Ryukyuan* Music

Compose original music using the *Ryukyuan* scale.

Column 2 # Travelogue in Japan ②

No. _____ Name _____

Write a brief travel guide about Japanese traditional crafts from Chubu, Kinki, and Shikoku.

Name of the traditional craft:

_____

Illustration or photo:

Travel guide: _____

_____

_____

_____

_____

Haiku to the World

No. _____ Name _____

My Haiku

Imagine the four seasons or a landscape.
What comes to your mind?
Brainstorm ideas and refine expressions.
Let's write Haiku.

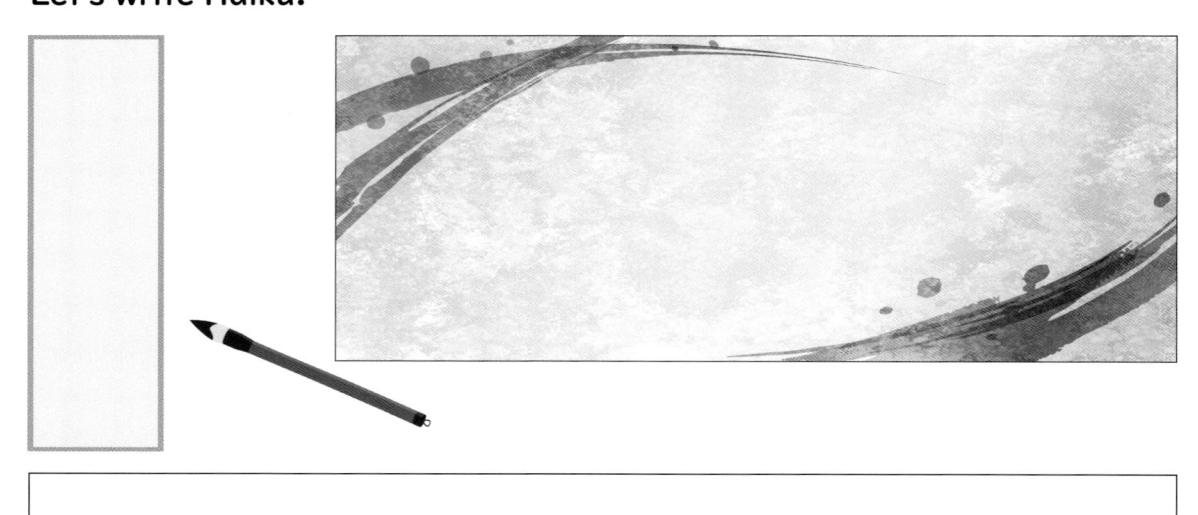

Mizuhiki

No. _____   Name _____

My Mizuhiki Design

1. Write the type of mizuhiki you will make:

Type (keychain   earrings   hair accessory   others)

2. Write the color(s) you will use:

Colors (   )

3. Write the kind of knot you will use:

Knot (kano knot   Awaji knot   ume knot   others)

4. Design your mizuhiki here:

No. _____   Name _____

Write a brief travel guide about Japanese traditional crafts from Chugoku, Kyushu and Okinawa.

Name of the traditional craft:

_____

Illustration or photo:

Travel guide: _____

_____

_____

_____

_____

_____

Japanese Curry

No. _____ Name _____

My *Yakuzen* Curry Recipe

Make curry with spices.

1. Make some notes about common health problems that you know.

2. Look up the spices that are effective for curing those health problems.

	Spice	Effect
1		
2		
3		
4		
5		

3. Write the best curry recipe to help cure one of those health problems.

Karate

No. _____   Name _____

Dojo-*kun* in English

Write the Karate dojo-*kun* in English.

How to write the dojo-*kun*

Seek perfection of character.

Follow the path of sincerity.

Put maximum effort into everything you do.

Respect others.

Develop self-control.

Travelogue in Japan ④

No. _____   Name _____

Write a brief travel guide about interesting traditional crafts around the world.

Name of the traditional craft:

_____

Illustration or photo:

```
┌──────────────────────────────────────┐
│                                      │
│                                      │
│                                      │
│                                      │
│                                      │
│                                      │
│                                      │
│                                      │
│                                      │
└──────────────────────────────────────┘
```

Travel guide: _____

_____

_____

_____

_____

_____

Fermented Food

No. _____ Name _____

Making Fermented Food

Present your experience making fermented food.

1. Decide which fermented food you will make.

2. Show the fermenting process and final product.

Mallorca Tiles

No. _____   Name _____

My Mallorca Tile

What kind of Mallorca tile do you want to make?

Design as symmetrical a pattern as possible.

Glossary

Lesson 1　Picture Candles

ancient time　古い時代、古代

reasonable　値段が安い

flickering flame　ゆらめく炎

characteristic　特性、特徴　[類義語] feature

obtain　得る

rush　イ草

soak　ひたす

feature　特徴　[類義語] characteristic

accompany　添える

stay lit　炎が静止している状態

region　地方、地域

bloom　花が咲く

peony　牡丹の花

chrysanthemum　菊の花

material　材料、物質

thick/thin　厚い／薄い

precious commodity　貴重なもの

rarely　めったに〜ない

Lesson 2　The Furoshiki

exist　現存する

used　使用された

travel　旅する

sell　販売する

increase　増加する

reduce　削減する

wrap　包む

fabric　布地

traditional　伝統的な

costume　衣装

public bathhouse　公衆浴場

family crest　家紋

merchant　商人

advertisement　広告

environmental concern　環境問題

plastic pollution　プラスチック汚染

sustainable　持続可能な

versatility　多様性、汎用性

reusability　再利用可能性

Column 1　Travelogue in Japan

bentwood container　木を曲げて作った容器（曲げわっぱ）

ancient ruin　古代遺跡

thinly peel　薄皮

Akita cedar　秋田杉

sturdy　頑丈な

900 degrees Celsius　摂氏 900 度

prevent rusting　さびない

involve gathering　集めることを伴う、含む

color scheme　配色

invent　考案する

manufacture　製造する

embroider　刺繍する

Lesson 3　The Namahage

ogre　鬼

typically　一般的に

refer to　〜のことを指す

blister　水ぶくれ

straw and linen　藁とリネン（麻）

shin guard　すね当て

pail　バケツ、桶

shout　叫ぶ

make loud noises　大きな音を立てる

lazy　なまけものの

break one's leg　足を骨折する

scared　怖がる

annual event　年中行事

take place　行われる

develop　（水ぶくれが）ひどくなる

avoid　避ける

behavior　行動

scary　恐ろしい

heartwarming　心温まる

swear　誓う

similar　似ている

smear mud　泥をぬる

chase children　子どもたちを追いかける

hand-carved mask　手彫りのお面

horn　角

fur cape　毛皮のマント

bless couples　カップルを祝福する

register　登録する

ritual　儀式

in common　共通に

Lesson 4　The Sanshin

be used　使用される

be categorized　分類される

genre　ジャンル

neck　棹

body　胴

tuning peg　調弦ペグ

craftsman　職人

musical scale　音階

pluck　はじく

snakeskin　蛇皮

bridge (*uma*)　ウマ

solfège　ソルフェージュ（音階唱法）

folk song　民謡

J-POP　日本のポピュラー音楽

Column 2　Travelogue in Japan

fade　色あせる

bendable　曲げることができる

calligraphy　書道

gorgeous　豪華な

practical　実用的な

be influenced by Buddhism　仏教の影響を受けている

gentle yet firm breeze　穏やかでありながらしっかりとした風

knife blade　刃物の刃

free forging　自由鍛造

method　方法

hammering　鍛造

instead of molds　鋳型ではなく

sword　剣

establish　建てる

lantern　灯篭

pillar　柱

assemble　組み立てる

dye　染料

tin　錫

copper　銅

copperware　銅器

molten metal　溶かした金属

mold　型

Lesson 5　Haiku to the World

poetry　詩

contribution　貢献

compose　作成する、作詞する

bloom　花盛り

come to one's mind　〜の心に浮かぶ

waterfall　滝

warbler　さえずる鳥

emotion-evoking scene　感情を呼び起こす情景

linger　余韻が残っている

refine　洗練する

phonology　音韻論

awareness of language　言語への目覚め

morae　拍（mora）の複数形

breeze　そよ風

Lesson 6　Mizuhiki

gift envelope　祝儀袋

delicately knot　繊細に結んで作る

generation to generation　世代から世代へ

artisan　職人

hand down　伝える

engagement ceremony　婚約式

crane　鶴

sympathy visit　お悔みの訪問

Buddhist rite　仏教の儀式

somber occasion　厳粛な場

undone　ほどける

long-lasting relationship　長く続く関係

weave　織る

athlete　アスリート

demand for　〜に対する需要

decrease due to 〜のために減少する

dramatically 劇的に

surprisingly 驚くほど

ornament オーナメント（吊るす装飾品）

souvenir おみやげ

Column 3 Travelogue in Japan

blur ぼかす

bubble 泡

be introduced from 〜から伝わった

forehead おでこ

range 種類、範囲

Heike clan 平家の家系

Lesson 7 Japanese Curry

cuisine 料理

flavored 味つけされた

variety of spices さまざまな香辛料

introduce 導入する

adapt 取り入れる

European-style stew ヨーロッパ風のシチュー

emerge 出現する

kampo medicine 漢方薬

instant curry roux インスタントカレーのルー

packaged curry product パッケージされたカレー製品

urban area 都市部

sauté ソテーする

brown 焦げ目がつく

remove from pot 鍋から取り出す

chopped carrots 刻んだ人参

bring to a gentle boil 弱火で煮る

simmer 煮込む

stir occasionally 時々かき混ぜる

soften 柔らかくする

Lesson 8 Karate

effective 効果的な

emigrate 移住する

offensive/defensive 攻撃的な／防御的な

recite 朗読する

principle 原理、原則、主義

apparently 〜らしい

martial arts 武道

element 要素

indigenous 固有の

adopt 採用する

refer to as 〜と呼ばれる

weapon 武器

unarmed combat 非武装戦闘

literally 文字通り

widely acknowledged 広く認められている

aspect 側面

philosophy 哲学

self-discipline 自己規律

practicality 実用性

emphasis 強調

evolve 進化する

diverse 多様な

guiding principle 指導原則

follow 従う

fundamental 基本的な

commitment 決意、誓い

rough draft 下書き

sincerity 誠実さ

Column 4 Travelogue in Japan

whale 鯨

waste 捨てる

handicraft 手工芸品

whisker （鯨の）ヒゲ

bone 骨

whalebone 鯨骨

baleen （鯨の）ヒゲ板

sperm whale マッコウクジラ

suitable flexibility 適度な柔軟性

highly valued 高く評価された

hairpin かんざし

tea coaster ティーコースター

dessert plate デザート皿

fishing rod 釣竿

ear cleaner 耳かき

backscratcher 孫の手 (magonote)

shoehorn 靴べら

local toy 地元のおもちゃ

whale ship　鯨船

actual whale　実際の鯨

fisherman　漁師

souvenir　おみやげ

wait at home　家で待つ

Lesson 9　Fermented Food

chemical process　化学プロセス

microorganism　微生物

beneficial effect　有益な効果

enhance　向上させる

nutritional value　栄養価

shelf life　保存期間

improve　改善する

gut health　腸の健康

antioxidant level　抗酸化物質のレベル

moisture　湿気

oxygen　酸素

fungi kingdom　菌界

aspergillus oryzae　アスペルギルスオリゼ（こうじ菌）

enzyme　酵素

carbon dioxide　二酸化炭素

regulate digestion　消化を調整する

lower blood pressure　血圧を下げる

inflammation　炎症

canned food　缶詰食品

notorious　悪名高い

herring　ニシン

unbearable　耐え難い

fermentation process　発酵プロセス

indigo dyeing　藍染め

scrub　こする

vat　（染め）桶

oxidize　酸化させる

Lesson 10　Mallorca Tiles

Mediterranean　地中海

primarily　主に

export　輸出する

opaque　光を通さない、不透明な

translucent　透き通るような、半透明な

entirely　全面的に

renovated　リノベーションされた、改装済みの

symmetrical　対称的な

symmetry　対称

asymmetry　非対称

trapezoid　台形

octagon　八角形

oval　楕円

imitate　模倣する

the Victorian tile　ビクトリア様式のタイル

reflect one's roots　ルーツを反映している

Zanzibar　国名 ザンジバル（アフリカ）

tomb　墓

specific technique　特有の技法

glaze　釉薬

clay slab to create an outline　粘土板で輪郭を描く

oil-based pigment　油性顔料

repel the oil off　油をはじく

the time civilization arose on Earth

地球上に文明が誕生したとき

CLIL 英語で伝える日本の伝統文化・伝統工芸

2025 年 2 月 20 日　第 1 刷発行

編著者	伊藤由紀子（いとう　ゆきこ）
	中田葉月（なかた　はづき）
著　者	竹内ニコール・マリー（たけうち　にこーる　まりー）
	柏木賀津子（かしわぎ　かづこ）
編集責任者	笹島茂（ささじま　しげる）
発行者	前田俊秀
発行所	株式会社　三修社
	〒 150-0001 東京都渋谷区神宮前 2-2-22
	TEL　03-3405-4511
	FAX　03-3405-4522
	振替　00190-9-72758
	https://www.sanshusha.co.jp
	編集担当　永尾真理

印刷・製本	日経印刷株式会社
DTP	藤原志麻
表紙デザイン	岩泉卓屋
イラスト	zoi

© 2025 Printed in Japan ISBN978-4-384-33539-2 C1082